KEEPING
MORAY EELS
IN AQUARIUMS

Phil Purser

www.tfhpublications.com

T.F.H. Publications, Inc.
One TFH Plaza
Third and Union Avenues
Neptune City, NJ 07753

This book has been published with the intent to provide accurate and authoritative information in regard to the subject matter within. While every precaution has been taken in preparation of this book, the author and publisher expressly disclaim responsibility for any errors, omissions, or adverse effects arising from the use or application of the information contained herein. The techniques and suggestions are used at the reader's discretion and are not to be considered a substitute for veterinary care. If you suspect a medical problem consult your veterinarian.

Library of Congress Cataloging-in-Publication Data
Purser, Phillip.
Moray eels in the aquarium / Phillip Purser.
p. cm.
Includes bibliographical references and index.
ISBN 0-7938-0566-X (alk. paper)
1.   Morays. I. Title.

SF458.M67P87 2005
639.3'743--dc22
2005005298

Dedicated to the care and well-being of companion animals for over 50 years.
www.tfhpublications.com

To Johnny Hickman, who taught me that "If you want to change the world, shut your mouth and start this minute."

And to Dr. Jonathan Evans, who taught me that some aspects of life are important, but "the rest is just a sideshow."

Thanks.

Contents

Introduction

From the days of my childhood when I watched one nature documentary after another about moray eels on public television, right up until the present day, these bizarre fish have long captivated my imagination. I drew pictures of them, sought them out at public aquariums, and when I was at last old enough to care for it, I bought one for my marine aquarium. He was a two-foot long Snowflake Moray that I named Spartacus. The black and white mottled animal lived for only six months, as I afforded it less than perfect care, and I was infinitely sad the day old "Sparty" passed into that Big Aquarium in the Sky. In the end it seemed like there were more questions than answers. What went wrong? What could I have done differently? Now, nearly 20 years later, I present you, dear reader, with this book, a collection of my experiences in moray husbandry, so that all the other little Spartacus's out there can have a longer and happier life than my first one did.

Born from the knowledge that there are many, many other marine hobbyists who share my love for the morays, this book is intended to be the answer to the question, the solution to the problem, the salve to the tender wounds that will certainly arise in moray keeping again. As much an educational text as a practical one, this book also intends to prepare (as well as possible) the hobbyist who has yet to purchase a moray, as well as to give wise council to the hobbyist already beleaguered by the nuances of moray keeping. Ultimately, I hope that my experiences, both good and bad, can help any moray hobbyist to avoid the same errors and pitfalls that ensnared me over the years, making your marine endeavor as fulfilling as possible, as well as ensuring your moray lives the best, longest, and most comfortable life possible while under your care.

So don't be afraid to wear this book out. Get it wet. Dog-ear the pages, bend back the spine, and maybe tear a corner or two. Above all else, use it. Make a reference tool of it. Keep it handy and keep it open, for in the end, your moray, your patience, and your wallet will thank you.

1

Moray Eels in the Wild

The veil of midnight hangs dark and heavy over the Indo-Pacific, blackening the waters beneath. Only the frail rays of a summer moon pierce the darkness. Under the waves, the diurnal creatures sleep, tucked away in the nooks and crannies of a silent reef, while the nocturnal animals go about their daily business. With eyes perched atop long stalks, a mantis shrimp emerges from its retreat and scales down the side of a coral. Capable of battering prey to death with its club-like claws, the shrimp searches for a sleeping damsel or other small fish. As it approaches a small, jagged hole in the reef, the shrimp's sensitive antennae twitch slightly, feeling the waters for its prey. The shrimp stops suddenly, its antennae sensing the vibrations of life. Something is nearby. Its senses heighten, anticipating the kill; the shrimp takes another fateful step towards the jagged cave. But that step would be its last, for out of a pitch black cave erupts the mottled head of a Blackspotted Moray, its jaws agape. The shrimp tries to flee, but the lighting speed of the moray will not be denied. As the crushing jaws and needle-like teeth of the eel impale the struggling shrimp and drag it back into the hole, the reef grows still and quiet once more.

Though to us it may seem like a scene out of *Jurassic Park*, this sort of thing is a daily, or should I say nightly, routine for so many species of moray eels. Morays are the prowlers of the deep, the wary snake-like hunters of the reef, and there are few hobbyists who can witness the brutal majesty of the morays and not feel drawn to their savage beauty. These fish are among the most bizarre in the seas; their cryptic lifestyle only adding to the cloak of mystery surrounding their existence and their place in nature. But morays do have their place in nature. They are valuable predators and scavengers whose hungry jaws eliminate the slow and the dying creatures of the reef environment, allowing the strong and swift to thrive, helping to further the cycle of life on the reef. And for this task, their bodies and lifestyles have evolved into a state of serpentine perfection; every part of the moray plays its role in making these animals what they are.

The family Muraenidae (the true morays) is comprised of nearly 200 species, though I am sure more species will be discovered as the Deep yields her secrets. Morays range in size from the diminutive Red-Faced Moray *(Monopenchelys acuta)*, which seldom exceeds 8 inches long, to the thunderous Giant Moray *(Gymnothorax javanicus)*, which may grow to nearly 11 feet long and may weigh 80 pounds or more. They come from all corners of the tropical and sub-tropical worlds, and are found in virtually every body of salt water between 30°N to 30°S Latitude. They have mastered life in nearly all marine environments as well, from the mangroves and grassy flats of southern Florida, to the Pacific atolls of the Bikinis and Micronesia, as well as the off-shore cliff faces hidden deep in the eastern Atlantic Ocean.

And if we, the ocean-loving hobbyists, are to have success when bringing a moray into our homes and into our lives, we must understand these animals as fully as possible. We must know them as we know ourselves. A working knowledge of a particular species' diet, habits, habitat, and behaviors in nature is key to meeting their needs in captivity, and avoiding disaster in the home aquarium. As is true with all marine creatures, a deep understanding of these animals will go a long way to ensure an enjoyable and long-lived relationship between the keeper and the kept.

Morphology: What Makes A Moray?

Long, muscular animals, the morays have a distinctly snake-like appearance, but they are indeed fish. Though they lack all traces of pectoral fins, morays sport fused dorsal and caudal fins that run from immediately behind the head to the tail (and back under the belly to the anus in some species). Couple this fin with their laterally compressed body and stream-line head, and it's easy to see how morays can be very powerful swimmers; their entire body form is made for ease of movement. Morays travel by a type of movement known as undulation. This rhythmic, slither-like motion only adds to their serpentine appearance, and is a very effective form of locomotion, especially for an animal that needs to come and go through such small, tight caves and nooks within the reef. The oar-like shape of the eel's tail pushes against the water on both sides of it and propels it through the

Morays are known for their "bulldog-like" grip, and the bite pressure alone that is exerted by some species is enough to break bone!

depths with speed and grace. Undulation also expends minimal amounts of energy, making the morays metabolically efficient; traveling the greatest possible distance while burning the least amount of calories.

All moray species are carnivores, and as such, they come equipped with a mouthful of specialized teeth for subduing prey. In fact, the teeth of each species tell us a lot about how that animal feeds. Species hailing from the genera *Echidna*, for example, have short snouts and small, peg-like teeth, designed for crushing the hard-shelled exoskeletons of their crustacean prey. Many of the larger eels, particularly those belonging to the genus *Gymnothorax*, have longer, sharper teeth with which the eel easily skewers its fishy prey. Some species, such as the Blackspotted Moray *(G. favagineus)* have not only sharp teeth lining their jaws, but also bony projections extending down from the roof of their mouth. These wicked pseudo-teeth, called vomerines, act as miniature spears, and aid the eel in grasping and hanging on to a thickly scaled or struggling fish. But such imposing dentition would be of limited use in a weak set of jaws. Far from weak, morays are renowned for their "bulldog" grip, and the bite pressure alone exerted by some species is enough to break bone!

Moray eels are completely scaleless animals. They have very smooth, sensitive skin. To compensate for a lack of scales, morays secrete a thick coating of protective mucus, which covers the entire body. Not only does this slimy coating guard against parasites and bacterial/fungal infections, it also lessens the chances of a predator getting a firm grasp on the eel, for as the jaws of a shark or grasping tentacles of a large octopus close around its body, the sleek eel may slip away, lubricated by its mucus coating. Hence the phrase "slippery as an eel." If its coating is abraded or damaged in an area, a healthy moray will quickly regenerate the damaged portion. On the other hand, a moray that is unable to produce its protective mucus will not be in this world for long.

The Senses

Like many nocturnal animals of the deep, the morays have exceedingly poor eyesight, and rely largely on their sense of smell to pinpoint prey. Animals that emit little to no odor, such as the parrotfish, are relatively safe from predation, while odorific species, such as damselfish, shrimps, and most crabs, are in for trouble when a hungry moray is on the prowl.

The moray's sense of smell is greatly enhanced by a most unique olfactory

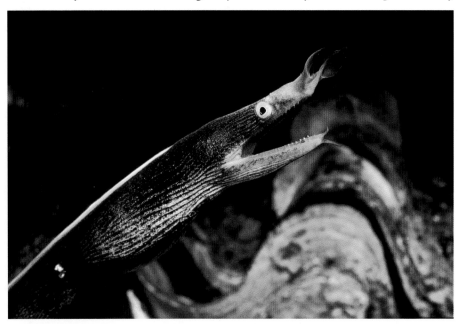

The Ribbon Moray (*Rhinomuraena quaesita*) employs a unique scenting strategy where it will actually turn in the direction of its prey based on which nare picks up a heavier scent.

adaptation. Funnel-like tubes extending from their noses and foreheads, known as nares, gather huge amounts of scent particles from the water around them. The anterior nares take in water, pass it over an olfactory sensing network situated beneath the skin of the snout, and expel it through the posterior nares, found on the snout just above the eye on both sides of the head. This one-way sensory system is far more efficient than our own noses, for it supplies constant information to the eel's brain, unlike our "breathe in, register information, breath out" strategy. And when, for example, the right-side set of nares picks up more scent particles than the left, the moray tracking its prey knows to turn right in its pursuit. The Ribbon Moray *(Rhinomuraena quaesita)*, in particular, employs this scent strategy, and has greatly enlarged nostril tubes resembling open flowers or trumpets, making for one awesome sense of smell.

Unlike most fish species, the morays lack a complete lateral line. The lateral line is a narrow network of nerves and sensory cells that runs along the flank on both sides for the length of the body, and tells most fish where they are in the water, how deep, and at what angle they are swimming. Morays do have a remnant lateral line running along both sides of their head, but this organ stops there. Considering that morays spend much of their time with only their head exposed, it's understandable that the lateral line needs to only exist on the head, which is the moray's "central control" for sensory information.

Where matters of vision are concerned, morays are not the sharpest knife in the drawer. With round pupils designed to take in only limited amounts of light, the morays can discern only poor degrees of color, but can readily distinguish intensities of light. The more intense the light, the less the moray is inclined to stay in the open. Morays can distinguish shapes with some proficiency at close range, but their true power of vision comes in detecting the nearby movement of their prey. Being able to see large shapes moving about alerts wild morays of the approach of predators, and tells captive morays that food is on its way (for with the approach of their keeper, often comes food). This association will likely become prevalent in captivity, and may result in a "puppy dog-tame" moray that seems happy to greet its keeper every time he or she draws near the tank.

While it is not well understood, morays also have a very keen sense of vibration-based hearing. By picking up the pulsation of an animal's heartbeat or its clumsy movements about the reef, the moray can attain a great deal of information about the creature such as size or type (be it fish, man, crustacean, another eel, etc.). The thrashing, struggling motions of an injured fish pulse through the water and

register with the moray just like an insect struggling in a spider's web. By keeping itself tuned into the frequencies of the sounds and vibrations around it, the moray knows exactly what is going on, despite its poor vision—just another item in the arsenal of sensory organs that make the moray a keen predator and devout survivor.

Perhaps the most striking aspect of the moray eel, and certainly the thing that most enthralled me as a child, is the way a moray will rest in its hole, leaving only its head and gaping mouth exposed, while constantly flexing its terrible jaws. The moray sports a menacing maw indeed. While this threatening display is certainly enough to frighten most divers, the eel hardly intends it as such. Morays have small, spiral-shaped gills with circular openings located directly behind the jaws on either side of the head. By rhythmically opening and closing its mouth, a moray is actually breathing; taking in water through the mouth and expelling it over the gills. So a moray's ominous mouth gesturing is the harmless equivalent of our chests rising and falling as we breathe in and out. This mouth-gaping gesturing is more pronounced in some species, and less in others. The Green (*G. funebris*) and Giant Morays are renowned for this behavior, and are typically the object of much attention for it, often gawked at both in the wild by reef divers, and in public aquaria by scores of mesmerized children (and me).

As can be imagined, the morays also have an excellent sense of touch, and navigate much of their way about the reef by keeping some point of their body in constant contact with the coral around them. Since open water brings many dangers (barracudas, sharks, etc.), the cunning moray will stay close to the reef at all times. When hiding in a hole or cave within the reef, the moray will also pick a tight-fitting home, in which its body touches its rocky surroundings on almost all sides. This gives assurance of safety to the moray, as tight quarters mean no sneak attacks from behind by hungry predators.

The Art of Survival

Although very little is known about moray breeding behaviors, it can safely be assumed that these eons-old animals have a highly effective mode of reproduction. All morays are oviparous, meaning they lay eggs. During a sort of underwater courtship dance, males swim alongside a receptive female and expel sperm into the water column at the same moment that the female expels her eggs. This moment of fertilization is very brief, though the dance leading up to fertilization may last for hours. The whole procedure may take place in the seclusion of a reef overhang

or sheltered cavern for some species or it may be an open-water endeavor for others. Once fertilized, the tiny eggs rise through the water to join the other microorganisms in the plankton layer. There the eggs will stay until they hatch into eel larvae. In no way resembling the adults they will soon become, the larvae, known as leptocephali, that look like long strips of translucent ribbon with a tiny head. The leptocephali will drift and feed in the plankton layer for an untold period of time before maturing. Upon maturation, the leptocephalus will take on all the morphological characteristics of an adult eel, and will leave the plankton layer, venturing back into the safety of the reef to start its new life as a fully formed, but still quite small moray eel. Despite having all its pieces in the right place, the newly metamorphosed eel is by no means sexually mature. The age at which sexual maturation occurs certainly varies between each species, and is not well known.

The adult-morph morays know how to defend themselves and flee from danger well. And during their earliest stages of mature life, the young morays must rely on all their instincts if they are to survive to adulthood. Once they return to the sea floor, young morays will immediately seek refuge within the reef, taking care to avoid anything and everything that is bigger than they are. Even other morays—perhaps ever their own parents—would certainly make a meal out of a young moray.

The cryptic patterning of this Dragon Moray (*Enchelycore paradalis*) enables it to "disappear" on the coral reef—even in bright daylight.

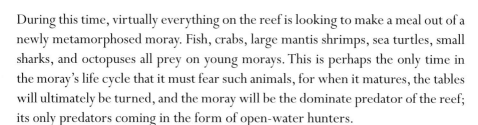

During this time, virtually everything on the reef is looking to make a meal out of a newly metamorphosed moray. Fish, crabs, large mantis shrimps, sea turtles, small sharks, and octopuses all prey on young morays. This is perhaps the only time in the moray's life cycle that it must fear such animals, for when it matures, the tables will ultimately be turned, and the moray will be the dominate predator of the reef; its only predators coming in the form of open-water hunters.

Of course, the moray is not just "thrown into the cold" and expected to survive. Quite the contrary, for moray eels come equipped with a wide arsenal of tools for survival; camouflage being chief among them. Shallow-dwelling species and those that frequent the living reef typically wear the brightest colors and the most elaborate patterns. Coral reefs team with life, thousands of little plants and animals cover every square meter of it, and amid this cornucopia of activity and color, the reef-dwelling morays are able to literally hide in plain sight—their vivid coloration and cryptic patterning blending perfectly with the mosaic of life around them. This camouflage strategy is perhaps best illustrated in the Dragon Moray (*Enchelycore pardalis*) and the Honeycomb Moray (*Muraena melanotis*), both of which can disappear, almost as if by magic, against the living backdrop of the reef.

The inverse of this is true for the deeper dwelling or offshore species. In the depths of the ocean, very little light can penetrate, so the best camouflage is afforded to the darkest, most subtly colored species. The patternless, olive-drab to brownish-yellow coat of the Green Moray, for example, render the animal virtually invisible—both to predator and prey alike—when hiding among the dark recesses of a deep-water cavern.

And when camouflage is not enough, the morays will not hesitate fight violently, putting those teeth and jaws into action to defend themselves from predators. When attacking an intruder, a moray will lock its powerful jaws into its victim, tie its body into a loose coil, and pull its head backwards through the loop, pushing against its prey with the coil. This maneuver affords the eel great leverage, and allows it to inflict incredible amounts of damage. Likewise, any animal that dares to molest a moray will soon be taught a painful lesson, as most morays will not hesitate to violently defend themselves. The speed at which a moray can execute this "loop attack" is startling.

Territory disputes among rival morays are a frequent source of violence; battles to the death are not uncommon. Unwelcome intruders, such as the errant hands of divers, may also suffer the wrath of an angered moray. Coastal hospitals around the world have admitted and treated scores of lobster and clam divers who foolishly

stuck their hand into a crevasse within the reef, and instead of coming out with the desired lobster or shellfish, they found their digits firmly and painfully locked in the jaws of a moray. These wounds were probably worsened by the knee-jerk reaction of the divers to struggle against the moray, pulling back their hand and further tearing their flesh on the moray's jagged teeth. Look before you leap, ladies and gentlemen. Look before you leap.

Severe moray bites should receive immediate medical attention, and be treated for secondary bacterial infections, which will almost certainly ensue. Never close a moray bite with stitches or staples, as closure can manifest internal bacterial colonization and possibly the onset of gangrene.

And if injured humans, with all our medicines and bubbling potions, have such a hard time healing from a severe moray bite, just imagine the damage suffered by marine predators. While diving in the Indo-Pacific near Borneo, I once witnessed an unidentified species of moray bite defensively against a small bamboo shark. The angered eel struck like a snake, locking its jaws onto the shark's snout for only a moment, then letting go. The shark reeled in pain, thrashing this way and that. Its head deeply perforated with a battery of teeth wounds, the shark swam upside down and sideways in jerky, involuntary motions. Before it drifted slowly back into the deep, I noticed one of its eyes was punctured, and hanging out of the socket. I looked back to the cave and saw the tip of the moray's snout protruding from the hideaway. Truly, these animals are not to be taken lightly.

Moray Look-A-Likes

The name moray applies only to one family of eels, though several other eel-like fish are often confused with the moray eels. The lampreys (family Petromyzontidae) and the hagfishes (family Myxinidae) are both very eel-like at first glance. They are long, cylindrical fish with laterally compressed tails, but their jawless heads and rasping tongues identify them as very different animals indeed. Likewise, the Oarfish (*Regalecus glesne*) has been mistaken by some for an eel. While this enormous fish (adults may exceed 55 feet long) is very elongate in body form and has a tall dorsal fin like that of the morays, it also has opercular gill plates and heavy scales.

Even within the anguillids, or "true eels," there are over 690 species in 19 families and 138 genera, so there's plenty of room for confusion! There are the Conger Eels (family Congridae), the Snake Eels (family Ophichthidae), and even the Spaghetti Eels (family Moringuidae), just to name a few. While all of these animals look similar at first glance, there are a few clues that tell if what you are considering for

Sometimes mistaken for a moray eel, the American Eel (*Anguilla rostrata*) is a true eel that spends much of its time in freshwater.

purchase is a true moray. For starters, the morays lack all traces of pectoral fins. The American Eel *(Anguilla rostrata)*, spends much of its time in freshwater, but matures into adulthood in the wide Sargasso Sea, and is frequently mistaken for a moray, though its pectoral fins are quite pronounced. Morays are also identifiable by their large, vaguely triangular heads and elongate, laterally compressed jaws. Hagfishes and lampreys have rasp-like tongues and sucker-lips for adhering to their prey, while Conger Eels have cartilaginous lips and horizontally compressed heads. Likewise, the Snake Eels bear pectoral fins and heavy scalation, as well as horizontally compressed heads and "lippy" mouths.

Fortunately, most reputable pet shops and online pet dealers specializing in marine fauna are not in the business of lying or trying to sell animals under false pretenses. If you are in doubt as to what eel you are looking at in a pet shop or online, get a second opinion or ask the Latin name, which will 99 percent of the time clear up all matters of confusion.

A lot can be learned about a moray just by understanding its Latin name. The name *Echidna nebulosa*, for example, is the scientific name of the Snowflake Moray. The genus *Echidna* means "spiky" in reference to the animal's blunt, spike-like teeth. *Nebulosa* means "cloudy" or "nebulous" in reference to the patchy, snowflake

pattern adorning the eel's skin. So literally, we might call it the spike-toothed cloudy-skinned eel, though I think Snowflake Eel is much better. Likewise, the *Gymnothorax pictus* breaks down into *Gymno* (Greek for "naked") and *thorax* (Greek for "chest") and refers to the animal's skin being scaleless. *(Pictus* means "spotted" or "speckled.") So put two and two together, and you get the naked-chest speckled eel, what we call the Peppered Moray. Beginners may have a little trouble (especially if you are new to the world of scientific nomenclature), but don't worry, you'll pick it up soon enough. Though it may sound strange, understanding the translation of your moray's Latin name is the first step toward truly understanding the type of eel.

Appearing in the fossil records some 135 million years ago, the first known ancestor of modern moray eels was not all that different from those species seen today. Fossorial morays lived and functioned similar to modern morays: they were of similar body style and hunted in much the same seek-and-destroy fashion do as modern morays. The teeth of this ancestral eel tell us that, like the eels of the present day, it was a meat eater and fearsome predator of the ancient oceans. Morays adapted in morphology and habits to life in the reef environment eons ago, and evolved very little except for coloration and slight variations in fin –placement. They were masters of survival then, and they still are today. Their bodies and senses have adapted so perfectly–in all ways–to a predatory lifestyle, that few reef prowlers can match their stealth and accuracy in the hunt.

The Moray's Niche

Having conquered virtually every body of tropical and temperate saltwater on the planet, most moray eels are reef associated, seldom thriving above or below the range of the reef. Other morays are demersal, meaning they can thrive in a range of depths, and may be found in tidal pools or several meters below the surface. Still others are totally benthic, living only at very great depths. Some moray species, such as the Freshwater Moray and Unicolor Snake Moray have even mastered life in brackish estuaries and in freshwater river deltas.

Most morays are reclusive creatures that seldom seek the company of other eels. They are hermitic predators spending their days in hiding, and enjoy the predictability of the reef around them. Some species stray about the reef continually to find food, but most return to their hole after foraging. As a general rule, a moray's hole is its home, and with the idea of home comes territoriality. And few undersea creatures will defend their territory with as much vehemence as the

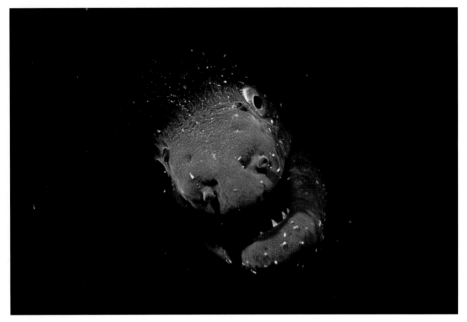

Morays typically inhabit dark, secluded areas of a reef or shipwreck where they patiently wait for prey to swim closely by.

moray eels. Of course, the degree of territoriality depends on both the species, as well as the individual in question. I have seen male morays battle to the death over a preferred hideaway, but I have also witnessed pairs, trios, or even more of the same species thrive communally in a single cavern. Much like people, each moray eel comes equipped with a distinct "personality," and much like our species, there is no concrete way to predict how an entire species will behave based on the actions of a few individuals.

Life at the Top of the Food Chain

Despite their specialized dentition, most morays are indiscriminate feeders, consuming just about anything they can fit into their mouths: shrimp, crabs, small lobsters, prawns, fish, squid, and especially octopuses. The relationship between moray eels and octopuses in the sea is one of pure hatred. Large octopuses are known to consume small morays, and adult morays are *renowned* for their appetite for octopus flesh. Even when an eel cannot eat the entire octopus, it will furiously attack the eight-armed creature, tearing at its flesh and at least coming away with a tentacle or two for its efforts. These two animals occupy similar niches in nature:

both dwell in caves and crannies in the reef and both are nocturnal predators. So encounters are common, and the outcome is typically fatal for the octopus.

Being the dominant predator on the reef throughout much of the world, moray eels may comprise more than half of all carnivorous species in a given ecosystem. In Hawaii, for example, which boasts of over 50 moray species, the total body weight of all morays is approximately equal to the weight of all other reef predators combined. Considering this animal's reclusive lifestyle and voracious appetite, it's easy to see how the morays are natural survivors. It is widely speculated that adult Green, Yellow, Giant, and Blackspotted Morays have few to no natural predators, and likely die of old age more often than not.

But not all lesser species on the reef are at risk. Rarely will the jaws of a moray close around a cleaner wrasse or cleaner shrimp. As their names suggest, these animals find food by "cleaning" detritus and tiny crustaceans off larger creatures. As powerful and menacing as a moray can be, it cannot brush its teeth or scratch an itch. That's where the cleaners come in. Sliding out of its hole, a moray will lie motionless and calm, while the wrasse or shrimp scours its body, picking off parasites, ridding its skin of burs of sand and grit, and even venturing into its mouth to pick old or snagged food out from between its teeth. The cleaner gets a free and safe meal (I'd like to see the predator bold enough to attack a shrimp that is in the mouth of a Green Moray!), and the moray gets a thorough and pleasurable cleansing of its mouth and body.

2

Morays and Man

L ike all animals and plants with which we share the Earth, our species and the morays have a long running history. We, the humans of this planet, through one culture or another, have hunted the morays, harvested them, worshipped them, eaten them, worn their skins, studied them, cultivated them, and kept them in aquariums for our own pleasures. The good news is that after all these centuries of humans interacting with morays, not a single species of moray eel is endangered or highly threatened. Mankind has a history of bringing about extinction to animals through our negligent actions, but I'm happy to say that morays are not among them. Let's keep it that way.

Morays in History

The notion of keeping moray eels in captivity is not a new idea; not by about two thousand years. Beginning around 200 B.C.E., the keeping of moray eels was viewed as a symbol of wealth and extravagance within the Roman Empire. Perhaps most notable among these early eel keepers was Licinius Muraena, who may have housed as many as 3,000-6,000 morays at once. (That's *a lot* of water changes!) So famous for his eel endeavors was Licinius Muraena, that the Latin family name of the morays, Muraenidae, was derived from Muraena's own last name. Vedius Pollio, who lived a full century after Muraena, is also remembered for his moray keeping. Close friend of Augustus Caesar, Pollio often hosted elaborate parties and festivals at his estate, where he showcased his morays in great bronze vats and ponds. At one celebration, held in honor of Caesar's recent victory in battle, Pollio

is recorded as having thousands of moray eels and lampreys on display.

Of course, these eels were not just for display purposes. Rome's leaders, elite citizens, and politicians (Pollio included) used vats and seaside ponds filled with morays for torturing insubordinate slaves. Lowered into the vat feet-first, the slave was immediately beset by hundreds of snapping jaws; the hungry, panicked eels sinking their teeth deep into the flesh, tearing muscle and chipping bone. Emperor Nero, in particular, favored morays as devices of torture. Criminals, slaves, and prisoners of war were often publicly executed at the behest of Nero, who offered ringside seats to his closest friends and associates. Death usually came from drowning, or suffocating under the mass of writhing eels. Some of the most notorious criminals, however, were tied at the shoulders to a catapult-like structure that allowed only their lower half to enter the vat. By keeping his victim's head well above water, Nero ensured the most prolonged, painful death possible--the biting eels rending the condemned man's flesh from his bones one mouthful at a time.

Moray eels even have their place in the bible. In his book of the same name, Matthew quotes Christ, who is speaking about the infinite love of God, saying: "What father, if his son asked for fish, would give him an eel?" The point of Christ's

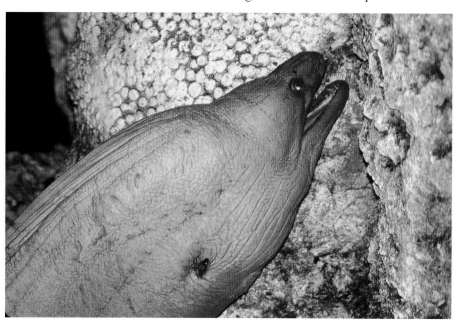

The Green Moray (*Gymnothorax funebris*) is one of the best-known species of Moray in the world. Early European seafarers would commonly pickle large Green Morays in barrels of vinegar or salt.

rhetorical question being that fish are good for the body, while eels, many species of which are toxic when consumed, are not. The full gravity of this parable is seen in the demise of King Henry I of medieval England. After eating an undercooked moray in the year 1135 A.C.E., old Henry contracted ciguatera poisoning, fell into a coma, and soon thereafter gave up the royal ghost. As time progressed, and man's exploits moved further across the oceans, our species and the morays have come into contact more and more frequently. Certain ancient Japanese customs held that an angered moray, when caught out of the sea, could breathe out lethal vapors. So when netted, a moray was immediately decapitated and its head thrown back into the sea before the ship and her crew could be poisoned. Other ancient Asian cultures, particularly those centered in present day Taiwan, held that a powerful and malicious eel god lived in the ocean, and often appeared in the form of a giant, black moray. Its appearance often heralded a cataclysm or other great misfortune.

Even the outlandish tales told by European mariners about ravenous, giant sea serpents have their own roots in moray biology. Captured Green and Giant Morays were often pickled in barrels of vinegar or salt. The preserved eels were then carried back to the mainland and put on display in traveling circuses and vagrant sideshows—for a price, of course. From the 1600s right up until the early 1900s, a many townsfolk throughout Europe and early America were duped out of their hard-earned coin just to catch a glimpse of one of these baby sea serpents.

And when it comes to harvesting natural resources (a skill at which mankind is particularly adept), man has certainly not overlooked the morays. Harvested both for food value and clothing, the morays provide a soft and rather bland flesh to worldwide markets. The Mediterranean Moray in particular is heavily relied upon for its value at the dinner table, and more than 50,000 tons of these animals were once collected annually throughout their range. Asian peoples also relish eel flesh, and in many localities throughout the nations of the Indo-Pacific region, moray eels factor heavily into subsistence fisheries, with an average of 35,000 to 40,000 tons of morays taken annually from the waters surrounding Japan.

Of course, not all morays are fit for human consumption (just ask Henry I). Many species contain accumulated toxins known as "ciguatera" or reef poisons that contaminate the animal's flesh. When eaten, ciguatera poisoning causes a range of symptoms: nausea, fever, excessive vomiting, dehydration, giddiness, body aches, coma, and in some cases, death. The most notable case of this comes from the Philippines. At a banquet there many years ago, fifty diners partook of a large moray and contracted ciguatera poisoning. All became ill, 12 fell into comas, and

two died. Within certain circles, there is speculation that ciguatera toxins may also exist in the saliva of contaminated species, and that mild poisoning may occur from a bite of one of these animals. Of course, this reputed semi-ciguatera poisoning is certainly the least of the foul side effects accompanying a moray's bite.

The moray eel's value to mankind extends far beyond the kitchen, however, for a many eels are harvested annually—legally and otherwise—for the leather trade. When cured properly, moray eel skin makes a fine-quality, supple leather that has been made into everything from belts and hatbands, to shoes, purses, and even cigarette cases. Coastal novelty shops also sell corked bottles containing pickled morays sporting the slogans: "Welcome to Florida" and "Greetings from Padrè Island." How morbidly disgusting! I wonder if in the souvenir shops of other galaxies, there are bottles containing preserved humans reading, "Nothing preserves your trip to earth like a pickled hominid!"

Even popular culture is inundated with morays. Who can forget Flotsam and Jetsam, the malevolent moray cronies to arch villainess Ursula in Disney's *The Little Mermaid*? Sadly, this pair of one-eyed eels was portrayed as purely evil, and perhaps left the movie's young viewers, who may have never before seen a moray, with a negative impression of these beautiful animals.

And, of course, the morays are harvested *en massè* annually for the ever-growing aquarium trade. Species from all corners of the globe make their way from the reef to the reef tank, but not all species are fit for captivity. Rather, the opposite is true, for the vast majority of moray species are regarded as useless and of no value to the aquarium trade. Either these animals are too blandly colored to attract any attention, or their diets and captive care requirements are so selective that only Mother Nature can successfully house them. Other species simply grow too large or do not adapt well enough to captivity to be considered by the average hobbyist.

But of the species that do show up in the aquarium trade, there are at least one or two, that are best suited for *every* hobbyist. Like a key in a lock, there is the right eel for the right hobbyist. "Right" in terms of how long-lived, healthy, and happy the moray will be under the keeper's care, and also "right" in the level of enjoyment and satisfaction gleaned by the keeper from his or her moray. And it is this matching of the right eel with the right keeper that this book hopes to achieve. At this point, if you're a veteran eel keeper, you may wish to flip to another chapter or read ahead to those topics you find most useful. But if you are a newcomer to the hobby–particularly if you are just considering a moray purchase–please lend me your attention for a moment more.

Morays in Your Home

The keeping of moray eels in home aquariums is one of the most rewarding and awesome endeavors that a marine hobbyist can undertake. These animals are ancient, yet highly sophisticated predators, and we fish keepers are truly blessed to have the opportunity and means to house such creatures. To witness in our own homes the savage majesty of the morays—the top predators of the reef—hiding, swimming, breathing, hunting, and living almost exactly as they would in nature is, a spectacle equaling the flight of a bald eagle or an Alaskan grizzly bear pawing a salmon from a river. The natural world has many gems and jewels to offer mankind, and the conscientious keeper who maintains his or her moray as best he or she can, truly receives one of nature's finest treasures. These animals are long-lived, stunningly beautiful, and each one seems to have its own personality. Some are aloof or distant, shying away from the approach of their keeper, while others seem to welcome the hand that feeds them. Some may live for decades almost oblivious to their surroundings, acting as if they are still living on a seaward reef in the Indo-Pacific. But the one thing about morays is they are never dull. How could a long, serpentine predator, its mouth agape in hungry anticipation of an impending meal, ever be anything less than exciting? We keep morays because of their uniqueness and because they embody the strangeness of the untamed Deep and because their alien movements and bizarre habits remind us—each and every time we pass by the tank—that we are but one species in the broad spectrum of exotic, curious, and precious life-forms that call this planet home.

3

The Moray Tank

Not just any aquarium is suitable to house a moray. These fish are masters of escape, haters of sunlight, devourers of tankmates, and topplers of unstable rocks, so there are a few considerations that must be made before adding a moray into your aquarium. If you already have an established, mature marine tank and your wish to house an eel in it, then likely you'll have to make some modifications to accommodate you new pet, but the workload will not be too intense. If, however, you are on the path I was so many years ago and are just starting up a tank because you saw a moray in the pet shop and now wish to do whatever it takes to own one, then you've got your work cut out for you. On the plus side, your moray will have its own home that was custom built *just for it* from the ground up, so chances are both you and your moray will be exceedingly satisfied with the results.

Tank Size

Imagine you are walking down the street and you see a lady walking a Labrador Retriever. Around the dog's neck is a collar that is five sizes too small, and strapped around its back is a harness that is equally tiny. The dog hassles and struggles to breathe against the choking collar, and his fur is irritatingly raised around the edges of the nearly lacerating harness. "Hi," the lady says happily. "Like my dog? I got him just last month and I love him to death!" You look at the lady and marvel at how cruel and ignorant she must be to shackle her beloved pet in such painfully tight constraints. Someone needs to tell her how to properly collar and harness her poor dog!

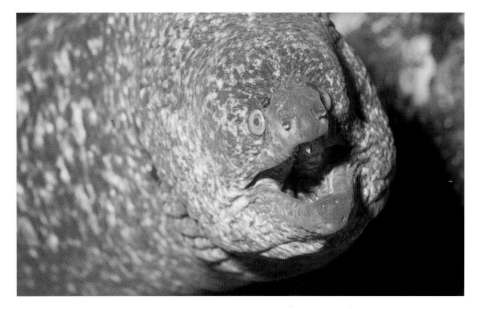

Many morays need large aquariums in order to thrive in captivity. Keep in mind that the aquarium should be *at least* two times as long as the moray's total body length.

The same holds true for moray eels, but far too many hobbyists keep them in frightfully small enclosures. Though we may not pet them, or scratch them behind the gills, or roll playfully in the grass with our morays, they still don't deserve to be constrained in tiny quarters. Let's face it, morays are big creatures, and they need equally big tanks to call home if they are to thrive under our care.

But when I say "big tanks," I do not necessarily mean big in terms of absolute volume, for even though a very tall, thin, octagonal tank may hold 300 gallons and thus be considered a "big tank," it still may not grant a 24-inch long Snowflake Moray the room to stretch out. The prevailing dimensions are *length* and *width*, with height being the least of your concerns. This concept is actually true with many, many other species of both freshwater and marine fishes. Morays are, regardless of species, primarily bottom dwellers, so depth of the tank is of little concern in their daily lives. A tank should be at least two times as long as the moray's total body length, and as wide as possible. This will allow the moray plenty of horizontal swimming space and room to fully straighten and extend its elongate body. Morays that are not able to fully stretch out suffer undue stress, and normally do not live longer than a few years in captivity, even when all other tank conditions are perfect. Your best bet, in terms of long-term success with your eel, is to determine

which species of moray you wish to keep *before* purchasing the tank. Figure out that species' maximum adult length, and purchase a tank that can comfortably accommodate the animal throughout its entire life span.

Tank volume is, however, important in terms of stable water quality. One good bowel movement on the part of a Purple Mouth or Zebra Moray will produce a certain amount of waste, which we will call "*X*." Now I was never good in math, but this equation is really a no-brainer. *X* in a 20-gallon tank will be ten times the concentration compared to the same volume of waste in a 200-gallon tank. Therefore, larger tanks not only afford your moray room to swim and move, but also allow biological wastes more room to dissipate within the water column. So even though your eel may be a small one, remember that the larger its tank is, the less frequently you must conduct water changes—although you still *must* do water changes. The healthier and more ecologically balanced your tank is, the *infinitely* easier your moray husbandry will be in terms of work, expense, and pet longevity.

Small quarters also increase outbreaks of violence in the community tank. A moray with plenty of room to call its own might live for decades in harmony with its tankmates, while a moray of the same species that feels cramped or restricted in its tank is likely to lash out against anything that draws near. Not only are tankmates at a higher risk of fighting, but escape attempts will rise, as will potential bites to the keeper during routine maintenance, water changes, or feedings.

Tank Style

As long as the condition of horizontal swimming space is met, the exact style of the tank is of little importance, and may be as basic or elaborate as the tastes of the hobbyist's desire. I do, however, recommend a glass tank over an acrylic one, as micropores in the acrylic will become magnets for algae and detritus buildup. The pores are virtually impossible to clean, and will eventually inhibit the clarity of the acrylic. Over the years, scratches, cuts, and scrapes will also limit visibility within the tank. Barring accidental breakage, a glass tank is far superior. The shape of the tank is also of little importance. I personally have never used anything but standard, rectangular tanks, though friends and family have employed everything from convex-fronted tanks, which afford a great view from the front, but are badly distorted on the sides, to fully circular custom-made tanks that are true showpieces. Again, as long as the moray has no less than twice its own body length to swim and stretch out, any shape is fine.

A large surface area of open water at the top of the tank is also a major plus, as tanks with smaller open surface areas are prone to radical swings in water quality. Surface area allows for ample gas exchange, which is critical to a successful moray endeavor.

Lighting

Although the matter of lighting your moray's tank may seem simple at first glance, there are actually many things to consider before flipping that switch. First of all, you must decide which type of lighting is most agreeable to your moray's natural inclinations. You must also consider which style of lighting most accommodates your budget and aquarium setup. Getting the lighting right is a big step towards making your moray feel as comfortable as possible in its tank. Too intense or too frail lighting can unduly stress an eel. There are basically three types of lighting suitable for the moray tank.

Fluorescent Lighting

Florescent bulbs are long, cool, quite inexpensive, and easy to operate. Florescent technology allows for broad-spectrum bulbs that flood the tank with excellent lighting; they are easily the most popular types of bulbs among aquarists. Florescent bulbs fit into shiny metal fixtures known as reflectors, which only serve to channel and intensify the light entering your tank. Corals, fishes, and most invertebrates will do well under florescent lighting, as will morays that are active during daylight hours. In the old days, there were just standard florescent bulbs, but today there is a wide spectrum of fluorescents designed to meet the needs of just about every hobbyist. Full-spectrum florescent bulbs provide a high degree of quality illumination for reef tanks and corals, while blue-actinic bulbs generate a dawn/dusk effect within the tank, which is perfect for most morays. Within my own tank, I use a triple reflector, fitted with two high-intensity florescent bulbs and one blue-actinic "night cycle" bulb. This dual-purpose setup allows me to simulate a true day/night cycle in my tank. During the day, my coral polyps flourish under the high-intensity lights, and in the evening my Zebra Moray goes on the prowl under the blue-actinic bulb. Using strictly blue-actinic florescent bulbs will create a deepwater effect in the tank, which is great for deeper-dwelling morays such as Green and Yellow-Edged Morays. Florescent fixtures are the most long-lived of all the lighting apparatus; a high-quality florescent may burn for several years.

A mixture of actinic blue and white lighting will provide good illumination for most aquariums containing moray eels.

Mercury-Vapor / Metal Halide Lighting

High-intensity incandescent lighting such as mercury-vapor or metal halide lighting, which are the shortest lasting of all the lighting apparatus, provide a pseudonatural slant of light that is great for creating shadows within the tank. I liken this lighting to sunlight shining down into the water on a cloudy day. Not all types of bulbs used in these fixtures are intense enough for acceptable coral growth however, so you will want to investigate the use of these fixtures further before going out and buying one. Mercury-vapor lamps are good for general viewing in the fish-only tank while metal halide units are more commonly used as high-intensity lighting over reef aquariums.

Diurnal morays, and those species that naturally dwell in shallow water environments, may move under the light of a mercury-vapor lamp. Mercury-vapor lamps produce more heat compared to florescent fixtures, and need to be suspended several inches above the tank to prevent overheating the water. Mercury-vapor or metal halide units are the only style of lighting that can create the rippling effect within the tank, making the inhabitants look like they are truly resting under a rolling surf. I recommend using mercury-vapor lamps when housing the Mediterranean Moray (*Muraena helena*).

Keeping Moray Eels in Aquariums

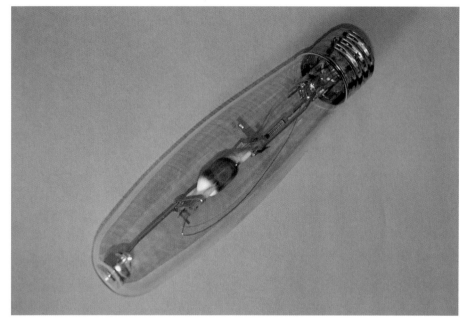

Metal halide lamps are by far the most intense type of illumination available to common hobbyists. These lamps have their pros and cons—as do all other types of lighting.

The most intense lighting of all is the metal-halide fixture. By broadcasting its powerful, full-spectrum rays into the tank, the metal-halide units can bring out the most beautiful hues and vibrant colors your tank has to offer. After viewing a reef tank under metal-halide for the first time, most hobbyists are sold forever on these high quality fixtures. Metal-halide is considerably more expensive to operate than either of the previous two styles, and is not advisable for most moray species, as its luminous rays are too oppressive for the eels' sensitive eyes, and the use of it tends to push most morays deeper into hiding. Metal-halide can, however, bring out the true beauty of such vibrantly colored species as the Dragon Moray *(Enchelycore pardalis)* and Jewel Moray *(Muraena lentiginosa)*. Metal-halide also burns hotter than either florescent or mercury-vapor, and needs to be suspended at least 8 to10 inches above the tank to prevent overheating the water. If you are planning to house your moray in a fish-only tank, then I recommend florescent or mercury-vapor lighting, however, if your moray will be a resident in a reef tank of living coral, then metal-halide is definitely your best bet for overall quality and aesthetic viewability. Just make sure that when using metal-halide fixtures, you provide your moray with extra-deep hideaways in which to escape the intense light.

Heaters

A heater (or heaters) is certainly a required fixture in the moray tank, as these animals thrive at temperatures of 72° to 80°F. But placing a heater inside the display tank is an all-around bad idea. Not only does it create an extra hole in the top of the tank (through which your moray will likely attempt escape), but it also presents a clear and present danger to the moray itself. While the tank water may warm gradually to a gentle 75°F, the filament of the heater gets quite hot; certainly hot enough to put some serious burns on a curious moray. When they come out at night to forage, many moray species may become entranced by the heater (particularly heaters with little red light indicators) and may nose at it and brush against it repeatedly, thereby marring their flesh with scores of tiny burns. These marks are at the least unsightly, and at the most prone to secondary infection.

Placing your heater in the tank's sump will eliminate such threats. This allows the tank's water to be warmed evenly outside the tank, while posing absolutely no threat to the moray (or any other organisms in the tank).

If placing the heater inside the tank is your only option, then the construction of an eel-proof cage around the filament is in order. Fit a thick plastic or nylon mesh sleeve over the filament, such that none of the tank's inhabitants can come into direct contact with the filament. Make sure the sleeve is made of a heat resistant material that will withstand the high temperatures generated by the heating coil. In-tank heaters should be of the fully submersible variety, such that only the cord of the heater exits through a pinpoint hole in the lid of the tank.

Substrate

When it comes to substrate, a little research into the natural habitat of the moray species you desire is in order. Most specimens will fare well on a shallow layer (between 2½ to 3 inches deep) of crushed coral, broken seashells, or a crushed coral/sand mixture, while others, such as the Tiger Reef Moray (*Scuticaria tigrina*), really love a substrate comprised entirely of sand. Some species, like the Undulated Moray, live among the rocks and corals of the living reef, and may not require any substrate other than the reef itself. If you do employ a purely sand substrate, it's best to wash the sand thoroughly in a large bucket before putting it into the tank. Prewashing will free the sand of any lightweight bits of biological debris, and will eliminate the sand dust (those powdery silica flakes) that can cloud water clarity and clog filter intakes. Unwashed sand is also hazardous to the gills of most fish, including morays. A light rinsing of crushed coral may help, but don't

go overboard, as calcium carbonate and silicate corals dissolve in freshwater; the sooner you place the coral in the tank, the better off you are, as repeated washes will lead to rapid breakdown of the coral. Crushed coral will dissolve over time, and will need to be replenished as needed.

Not only should you consider substrata based on the natural preferences of your moray, and your own aesthetic tastes, but also know that a healthy layer of substrate can go a long way in balancing the nitrogen cycle within your tank. Coarse-grained or very porous substrata create millions of tiny pockets within the tank floor. While these pockets may be too small for the naked eye to detect, they will provide great habitat for nitrifying bacteria, which will help to digest and breakdown biological wastes in the tank. Avoid very fine-grained sands or powdery crushed corals. Instead, look for larger, coarser grained items to help propagate these beneficial bacteria. As crushed coral breaks down and settles in a dense layer, the *Nitrobacter* pockets will diminish in size and number, thereby reducing the population of nitrifying bacteria. Replacing and replenishing the crushed coral will be periodically necessary to maintain these bacteria-pockets.

A final word on substrate, unless the species you desire specifically needs or requires a substrate other than crushed coral, I would recommend using solely

The soft, scaleless skin of morays can get scratched by substrata that are too coarse. Use caution and common sense when selecting the type of substrate that your morays will be resting on.

crushed coral. As this material breaks down, it raises the pH of the tank into the low 8.0s and goes a long way in continually buffering the tank. Unbuffered tanks, or those with uncrushed coral substrates, are much more prone to radical, sudden swings in pH, which can prove fatal to most moray species.

Caves & Hideaways

When it comes to hideaways in the moray tank--- more is better. Morays are reclusive animals that, in nature, spend most of their time tucked safely in a nook within the reef. Even when hunting, morays stick close to the sea floor or reef, seldom straying far into open water, as there they are exposed and vulnerable to attack by sharks or other predators. If this need for security is ignored or underestimated in the aquarium, there is little doubt that the moray, regardless of species, will stress, wither, and soon perish.

Place several hides of various sizes throughout the tank, as morays can be picky when it comes to choosing a home, and the more options it has, the better. Provide small hides as well as large, for morays, much like snakes, oftentimes prefer small, tight-fitting hides over larger ones. Because of their elongate form, eels feel most

Caves and crevices are a must in a moray's aquarium. Today, hobbyists have many options when choosing which decorations they wish to incorporate into their aquariums.

A Quick Note About Driftwood

The use of driftwood, or bogwood, in marine aquariums is not usually recommended. However, in setups housing moray eels, you can usually get away with using small amounts of this wood as tank décor. Be certain to never use it without first thoroughly soaking the pieces for several days. Doing this will help release excessive amounts of tannins. These tannins will cause the color of your water to become a yellow tea-stained color and may detract from the overall appearance of your aquarium. Soaking driftwood will also help ensure that it will sink when placed in your aquarium. It can be very frustrating to spend a good amount of money on a beautiful piece of driftwood only to bring it home, rinse it off, and have it float to the surface of your aquarium. Be sure to soak your new driftwood for at least three full days and periodically changing the water during that period.

secure when their body touches their retreat on all sides. And that snug, secure feeling is exactly what you're going for.

If opting for natural structures, such as rocks or corals, be sure that these items are secured within the tank. Never build a hideaway by stacking rocks or corals. Morays are powerful animals that can unsettle items within the tank, and should a pile of rocks shift or fall at the wrong moment, the result could be disastrous. Drill a small hole in the rocks and bind them together with nylon zip-ties. This method allows you to use your imagination in building structure for your eel (constructing elaborate networks of cave, ledges, coral atolls, etc.), while at the same time insuring against collapse and possible injury to the eel or damage to the tank.

While a custom-built network of caves and corals designed specifically for your eel may be effective as shelter and beautiful to the eye, it is certainly not the only option. Artificial items, such as clay pot halves and PVC pipes make excellent hides. If aesthetics are of little concern, a length of PVC immersed in the tank will likely become your moray's favorite hide. PVC is safe, durable, lightweight, and easily removed for cleaning. As your eel grows, simply provide another length of pipe of a slightly larger diameter.

Signs of an inadequately sheltered eel include listlessness, restlessness, loss of appetite, increased breathing rate, and erratic swimming at all levels of the tank. Under these conditions, the eel feels exposed and vulnerable. It has no idea that the confines of your aquarium guarantee its safety. Its natural defensive instincts are in a state of high alert and will stay that way until either the situation is remedied or

the moray perishes. Adding more or more suitable hides will quell this behavior and put your eel at ease.

Again, the exact moray species you wish to house will determine style and density of the hides your tank must have. The Zebra Moray *(Gymnomuraena zebra)*, for example, is a staunch reef-going species that thrives best in a tank tightly outfitted with one continuous network of caves and hideaways, while other species, such as Spotted Moray *(Gymnothorax moringa)*, require only a few, separated hides and plenty of open water in which to tool about.

Other Tank Furnishings

Many hobbyists enjoy placing other, nonliving items within the tank purely for aesthetic purposes. Seashells, glass marbles, unusual rocks, and other inert items can be added without any problems, as most morays seem oblivious to such things. Be warned that some rocks will break down in the water column, and can add minerals and calcium, which can throw off the balance of your aquarium. Never add items that have been shellacked, stained, or otherwise chemically treated in any way, for such items pose an extreme risk of contaminating the tank; perhaps lethally so. I've also seen driftwood in marine tanks on occasion, especially special

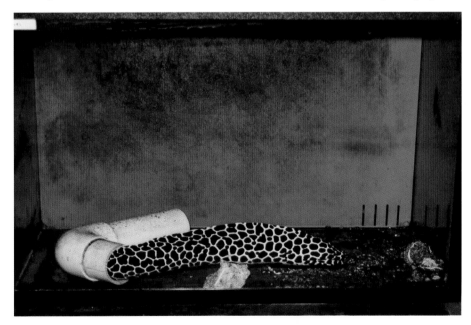

Sections of PVC piping can be used while your new moray is in quarantine. While unappealing to the eye, their functionality is top notch.

habitat tanks like mangroves and shallow lagoon setups. While most marine species have no need of driftwood, I do recommend using some if you have a marine or brackish setup for a Unicolor Snake Moray or Freshwater Moray. Just keep in mind, that as driftwood decays, it can drastically lower the pH of your tank and add to the levels of detrimental biomatter. Never introduce driftwood or shells into your tank directly from the wild, as doing so will also introduce any number of unwanted marine pests or parasites. First, scour such items with hot water, thus removing all loose debris and destroying all microfauna, and allow the items to dry in the sun for several days.

Tank Security

If you have a pen or pencil handy, you'll probably want to underline this next line, for you are about to read the golden rule of moray husbandry: EACH AND EVERY SPECIES OF MORAY EEL IS A MASTER ESCAPE ARTIST!!! It's true, more than half of all moray deaths in captivity are the result of the eel finding a gap or hole in the lid of the aquarium through which it can escape, fall to the floor, and dry up into a two foot long, $75 strip of eel-jerky. In their native habitat, morays are *constantly* wriggling in and out of tight crevasses and cracks within the reef, and this behavior will not disappear in the home aquarium. If anything, a restless or curious moray (especially those kept in cramped quarters) is more likely to explore the limits of its glass-walled home than one provided with plenty of room. Therefore, both to preserve the moray's life, and to protect your investment, it is critically important that you secure your aquarium. A tight-fitting, heavy glass lid is best for most species, though some modifications must be made if you house very large or overly strong species. Most glass lids have a strip of acrylic or plastic along the rear edge. This acrylic is often notched or manipulated to fit hoses, filter intake stems, and piping into the tank. Take special care to cut this acrylic to *exact, form-fitting* specifications so that no undue gaps are left. A general rule of thumb is that if a gap is half the width of the moray's head, it is too wide and may allow escape. If your lid already has gaps that are too large, these may be sealed using a nontoxic sealant such as hot glue, silicon, or spray-on foam.

Unusually powerful species, such as Green, Yellow, and certainly Giant Morays have a tendency to push open glass lids and wriggle through the opening. Prevent this by weighing the lid or securing it with suction cups (one on the top of the lid, and another on the side of the tank, bound together with metal hooks or stout cord). Some hobbyists employ multiple lids, using a dense milk crate or plastic

pegboard. Cut to the proper size, this material may be used to fill gaps in a glass hood. When used by itself, a milk crate lid allows for excellent gas exchange and the release of harmful vapors emanating from the tank. The only drawbacks to this open-air style of lid are that strong eels can push up the edges of the milk crate, and brittle or fragile crates can be broken outright by strong or boisterous species. I once lost an Undulated Moray when, during the coarse of its nightly activity, it jumped out of the water and burst through a narrow sliver of plastic grating adjoining my glass lid to the tank.

A tight-fitting metal or nylon mesh screen lid is also a viable option. If your tank is drilled or uses external filters, water return will flow easily though the mesh, and a jumping eel will not be injured when leaping against the soft nylon mesh. Mesh lids, like crate lids, also allow for a high degree of gas exchange. Especially when used in conjunction with a glass hood, a mesh screen can go a long way in preventing escapes. Use some creativity when securing your tank, and put yourself in the place of the moray. Could you find an escape hole if you were the moray? Seal all gaps, shore up all seams, tighten all lids, and fortify your lid as best you can.

Another consideration of security is not what it takes to keep the eel in, but also to keep any children *out*. If you and I, dear hobbyist, are so taken by these unusual animals, then a child will be *positively spellbound* by them. Fitting a heavy, lockable lid over the top of tanks containing potentially hazardous or traumatogenic species is not only in the best interest of safety, but a well-crafted, stained wooden hood is a great way to conceal all those ghastly glass, mesh, and crate lids!

4

Moray Compatibility

The final step, and perhaps the most practical, before purchasing your moray, is to understand the basics of morays and their tankmates. After all, where is the sense of purchasing a $70 moray, only to have it devour, harass, injure, or cripple the $700 of livestock already in the tank? Likewise, no sane hobbyist would spend that $70 on a moray, only to find it bitten or mauled to death the next morning; slain in a fray with an aggressive tankmate. If you have not done so, I urge you to read about and research morays in the wild to better understand how these animals will likely behave in your tank. A good, working knowledge of morays and their niche in nature will go a long way in curbing possible disasters in the aquarium.

The Nature of the Beast

The first thing to realize is that all morays are predators. They survive by killing and eating the animals around them. This killing instinct will not go away just because we feed them cut foods and give them cute names (like Spartacus), and as any veteran hobbyist will tell you, keeping a predatory animal adds a whole new dimension to maintaining the aquarium. In the wild, morays are generally staunch loners. They do not school as other fish, nor do they tolerate the company of many other species—except for each other occasionally. They are reclusive and retiring when comfortable, but savage when defending themselves and when hunting. We must come to terms with the reality of these truths, and not let our lavish tastes for a little of this and a little of that in the aquarium lead us to mix incompatible species then complain, or swear, or abandon the hobby when one animal eats the other. It's not fair or ethical to endanger the lives of our pets simply because we really, *really* want to mix certain species. Even when we're fairly certain that some species will coexist well (or have been coexisting well for a while), it's still a very real possibility that you'll turn on the light one morning only to find your Miniata Grouper or Titan Trigger gone, and a very large lump in the belly of your moray. Such is the nature of the predator.

Morays in the Reef Tank

When introducing a moray eel into a pre-existing reef tank, it is obviously best to choose a species that frequents coral reefs in the wild, as such an animal will be comfortable under the prevailing conditions of your tank. Secondly, you'll want to consider the needs of the reef itself. Tanks supporting elaborate colonies of tubeworms, delicate corals, anemones, and fragile sponges may suffer under the movements of an exceedingly large or boisterous species. Adult Green, Yellow, Yellow-Edged, and Undulated Morays are all likely to wear down, break, or crush the tiny living things in your reef tank. Larger morays also produce larger amounts

Various nooks and crannies are excellent spots for the retiring moray. Of course, check to make sure that the species you are interested in is reef-safe *before* placing it in your reef aquarium.

Mixing morays of different species is generally not a good idea as violence between the species, among other things, often leads to death or serious injury for one or both parties.

of nitrogenous wastes, which can seriously damage all life on the reef through biological contamination. Coral polyps and other minute organisms are even more sensitive than morays to nitrogenous wastes. So a smaller moray species may be desirable in such delicate ecosystems. If you have a very large reef tank, however, perhaps something over 500 gallons, you might find that keeping a large moray with lots of small crustaceans and tiny fishes creates a unique dichotomy, as the moray will likely not view these minuscule items as sources of food, but will swim among them daily without incident. The theory behind this behavior is that these small crustaceans and tiny fishes will not warrant attack by the moray because the energy that the large eel will exert in the attack will be more than the energy received from the meal.

Likewise, you will want a species that will not devour any of the sessile or tiny motile invertebrates within the reef tank. It is best, therefore, to look to the toothier morays, for these slender-jawed animals tend to favor fish and cephalopods over urchins and cleaner shrimps. Species hailing from the genus *Echidna* and the singular species of *Gymnomuraena* have shorter, peg-like teeth, and are specialized in dining on shelled inverts, so the mixing of these species with reef-going inverts is, in most cases, not a viable option. Good reef-safe moray species include the

You can easily see the long, sharp teeth that make the business end of this *Gymnothorax fimbriatus* look so menacing. Now imagine if you were a damsel!

Unicolor Snake Moray, Jewel Moray, and small Mediterranean and Blackspotted Morays. Bear in mind, however, that introducing *any species* of moray into a tank containing motile inverts is a calculated risk. Most small fish in an invert tank are also potential meals to moderately sized morays. Clownfish that live continually in and near their host anemone may be safe if that anemone is positioned well away from the moray's chosen lair.

Morays in the Fish-Only Tank

Adding a moray eel to a fish-only tank is considerably trickier, as even crustacean-loving species will still devour a sleeping fish if given half a chance. If currently housing damsels, clowns, tangs, dwarf angels, or any other species under 6 to 10 inches in length, then chances are it will end up on the menu sooner or later. Many hobbyists think that if you keep your moray well fed, it will not dine on its tankmates. This is not true. Many hobbyists have also made the false assumption that aggressive fish will not allow themselves to be eaten. Again, not true. Since morays are quite docile most of the time (just quietly resting in their caves), they are subject to bites, nips, and continuous pestering by aggressive fishes. This is not only terribly unfair to your moray, but to the aggressive fish as well, for when

Many species of parrotfishes are gorgeous, but only the larger ones are suitable for the moray aquarium. Their sleeping habits invite predation by the ever-curious moray during its nighttime forays.

a moray gets hungry, it's most likely going to strike in the black of night, when the aggressive fishes are sound asleep, making for a lose-lose situation. For these reasons, I never mix morays with triggers, dwarf angels, and especially not with large wrasses, which in my opinion are some of the worst hecklers in the ocean. Some species of triggerfish may coexist with morays, but many have a tendency to nip at the moray's fins and eyes when hungry. The graceful, undulating motions of a moray are often too tempting for a hungry trigger to resist taking a bite out of the eel's fins or flanks.

The best way (and even this is not a 100 percent guarantee) to mix fish and morays is to play by the rules of nature. Mix smaller, crustacean-eating morays with larger, non-aggressive fish species that are naturally protected either by size or other means. Groupers, Pompanos, and small Jewfish are usually protected by their sheer bulk, and often make good tankmates for morays in very large enclosures. Chemically armed fishes are perhaps the best tankmates for morays. Lionfishes, puffers, porcupine fish, and especially the Coral Catfish bear poisonous fins and vibrant coloration, which warn all potential predators to stay away. In nature, morays recognize the warning-colors and prickly shape of these species and seldom attack. In captivity, these animals typically demonstrate a healthy

Mixing Morays

In a sentence: Don't do it. Mixing different species of morays or even multiple individuals of the same species is not a good idea, no matter how you cut it. Stress increases, nitrogenous waste skyrockets, and violence may eventually claim one or both morays. If you insist on attempting this then you should know that there are some species that tend to mix better than others, and there are some clever tricks that make mixing these animals possible. While I do not recommend mixing morays, the following list will help any hobbyist who is bent on doing so.

- Mix morays of approximately equal size.
- Supply at least three hides for each moray.
- Only mix morays in a tank of 200+ gallons; 1000+ gallons for very large species.
- Introduce both animals to the tank at the same time.
- Only mix docile species together.
- Sufficiently feeding each animal may reduce the likelihood of it devouring the other.

If introducing a new eel into a tank with a resident eel, remove the resident moray to a quarantine tank, rearrange the tank's furnishings dramatically then add both morays to the tank. Sometimes this may curb the resident's territorial behavior and allow both morays to establish themselves within the "new" tank.

Introduce both morays to one another when they are as young as possible, for juveniles may coexist for life, while adults will sooner see each other as rivals, and may battle to the death.

Only mix fish eaters with fish eaters, and crustacean eaters with crustacean eaters (i.e., two morays belonging to the same genus). For example, two Snowflake Morays will likely coexist better than a Snowflake and an Undulated Moray.

degree of respect for one another, and may coexist peacefully for decades. All of the aforementioned fish are not aggressive, and will not likely pester your moray.

It's Lonely at the Bottom

A final rule of moray compatibility is to avoid mixing fish species that will naturally stay in close proximity to your moray. Different fish species have different lifestyles, and will thrive at different levels of the tank. Morays, obviously, are bottom-dwellers, seldom leaving the safety of their structure or venturing far to forage. But when something comes too close to the eel, watch out! Putting other

bottom-dwelling species in a moray tank is just begging for trouble. Sharks, rays, gobies, grammas, blennies, and other bottom-dwellers may well be killed, injured, or eaten outright by your moray, while large or powerful sharks might turn the tables, possibly killing your moray.

Upper and mid-level swimmers such as large sweetlips, hogfish, and angels spend most of their time out of the moray's domain and are less likely to be attacked. Likewise, lionfishes and groupers also usually stay a goodly distance away from the moray's domain, making them doubly suited to living with a moray. Situating the moray's retreats away from the rest of the activity in the tank may also curb fish loss, and the eel may also enjoy such peaceful, stress-free isolation. Distance from the rest of the tank's activity can make matters of feeding easier in that tankmates are less likely to seek out the eel's fare, and the moray is not so prone to bite a nearby fish, mistaking it for a tasty morsel of shrimp.

The only guarantee when dealing with morays and their compatibility with other life-forms is that there are no guarantees. Unpredictability is an ever-present side effect of housing one of these predators, and a newcomer to the moray hobby will soon learn that there are no hard and fast rules of compatibility. As soon as we

These small morays (*Echidna* sp.) will probably not even break the skin if they bite you.

establish a rule, a moray will find a way to break it. Bear in mind, also, that different species of morays will react differently with various tankmates. Remember that fish-eating morays do better in reef tanks, while crustacean-loving eels are less of a threat in the fish-only tank.

Treating a Moray Bite

When it comes to morays in the home aquarium, tankmates are not the only creatures that need to beware of the eel's vicious maw. All too often it is we hobbyists—usually out of carelessness—who become the victims of a moray bite. If you are bitten, resist the urge to pull away, as it is the sudden backward jerking motion of a panicking keeper that can turn a few mild puncture marks into a series of jagged, deep lacerations. Most moray bites are either the result of confusion or quick aggression on the part of the eel, and once it realizes that it has hold of you and not the shrimp it was expecting, it will likely let go. Bites inflicted defensively or out of fear are typically "strike-and-release" in nature; the moray seldom locks its jaws onto the object it fears. There is also some speculation that the five-fingered hands of a hobbyist, when viewed through the hazy eyes of a moray, closely resemble a small octopus—the favorite fare of many morays. If for

It is easy to see that a bite from this Dragon Moray (*Enchelycore paradalis*) could be very painful.

some strange reason the moray does not let go, simply raise your hand and the eel's head out of the water and hold it aloft until the oxygen-starved moray releases its hold and falls back into the tank. If this does not work, get someone else in the house to pour a small amount of liquor into the moray's mouth; the animal *will* release its hold.

In the case of mild bites, wash the wound thoroughly and check for any tiny shards of broken tooth that may be anchored in the flesh. Cleanse with a topical antibiotic and watch closely for any signs of infection. If the wound is more serious (perhaps inflicted by a large or very toothy species), a trip to the local emergency room is in order. Signs of a "serious" bite include excessive bleeding, deeply torn flesh, and severe, lasting pain. The mouth of most morays is a very nasty place where bacteria ride tall in the saddle, and a bite is like injecting your flesh with these hated microbial organisms. Treat under a doctor's care with antibiotics (both topical and oral) and X-ray the wound for internal or skeletal damage, as an adult Green or Blackspotted Moray can easily crack, pierce, or chip the bones of its keeper's hand—ouch!

5

Filtration For Your Moray Tank

Think back to the last time you went diving, if you've ever been diving, and remember how the undertow of the currents ebbed and flowed over the reef and how the life-giving flood of the ocean swept the reef clean of detritus and brought much-needed oxygen with every wave. If you do not dive, or have never been to the ocean, it is important to know that the constant surging of the ocean is perhaps the most powerful force on the planet, and it keeps the reef clean, healthy, and nourished on all counts. Without the push and pull of the tides, the reef would fester and stagnate, and all living things that call the reef home would soon perish in their own biological waste.

In my experience, nearly all of the problems in marine aquariums are caused by poor or inadequate filtration, which often leads to poor water quality. Morays—like all carnivorous species—produce copious amounts of nitrogenous wastes. Their excrement is protein rich and can quickly pollute even a very large tank, so it should come as no surprise that a successful moray endeavor will require a hefty amount of filtration. The style of filtration that you employ is of little importance as long as the turnover is *at least* 8 times the tank's volume per hour, and utilizes biological, chemical, and mechanical filtration, as described below. I recommend the use of canister filters and powerheads, as these items create some additional current within the tank. These filters also leave minimal gaps at the top of the tank, reducing the risk of escape by the eels. Bio-wheel style and hang-on filter units are also great choices, so long as adequate measures are taken to prevent escape attempts through the gaps they leave.

Biological Filtration

Biological filtration refers to the *living components* within the substrate, filter media, and water column that attack, breakdown, or devour the organic pollutants in the tank. Critical to controlling the nitrogen cycle, these living organisms, known as nitrifying bacteria (or *Nitrobacter*) consume the harmful nitrites in the water and convert them to relatively inert nitrates. Responsible for turning the "dead water" of an aquarium into the living, thriving, and healthy water akin to that found in the sea, biological filtration is the natural process by which all dead, organic items breakdown in the wild.

Biological filtration can be slow to develop, and is of limited power, as copious amounts of organic wastes (especially the amounts produced by large morays) can overwhelm the biological filtration in your system. When the buildup of these organics is so great that the biofiltration cannot process it all, the tank's water will be corrupted and the inhabitants will soon perish. Biological filtration will

Live rock is by far the best choice for balanced biological filtration, since it contains a wide array of aerobic and anaerobic bacteria.

eventually establish itself in your tank on its own, but can be (and should be) kick-started by adding the proper dosages of live bacteria to the tank. Commercially sold under any number of names, these living potions need only be poured into a newly established tank and allowed to flourish within the substrata and filter media. Older tanks, which may be experiencing spikes in ammonia or nitrites due to their new moray inhabitants, may also benefit from an occasional seeding of living bacteria.

Chemical Filtration

Chemical filtration is a non-biological process through which the harmful chemical components of the aquarium's water are chemically altered, made inert, or destroyed utterly. Using activated carbon and ammonia-absorbing chips (known as ammo-chips) in the media compartment of your filter are good examples of chemical filtration. As water rich in ammonia and nitrites passes from the aquarium and over these media, the carbon and ammo-chips react with the gases on the atomic level and form tight bonds that lock the offending chemicals into the media, thereby removing these harmful agents from the aquarium water. Chemical filtration is an excellent tool within the filtration system, and because

Activated carbon should be replaced frequently in order to ensure that it is consistently removing toxins and other organic and inorganic pollutants.

of all morays' sensitivity to buildup of ammonia, nitrites, and nitrates, chemical filtration is an absolute must in the moray tank. But the powers of chemical filtration alone are limited. While it can go a long way in removing dangerous agents from the water, it cannot remove the sources or the causes of these agents: the decomposing organic items.

Mechanical Filtration

The term "mechanical filtration" refers to filtration that physically removes the ammonia-causing debris from the water column; it comes in many forms. Foam, sponge, or dense-fiber inserts in trickle and canister filters act as fine seines, trapping organic matter suspended in the solution. These seines must be cleaned or replaced regularly, as the chemical by-products of this trapped refuse will still be circulating through the tank and filter system. Because of the copious amount of wastes produced by morays, I recommend using a high degree of mechanical filtration. Even devoting all the media compartments in a canister filter solely to

Large sumps allow the hobbyist to incorporate various methods of filtration. This sump is set up for efficient mechanical filtration by using a filter bag.

this purpose is a recommended. Put the coarse seining material at the top of the filter to trap the largest bits of debris and finer foam at the bottom to collect the smallest particles. By trapping the loose bits of waste and rotten food inside the filter, any harmful bacteria or fungi living among the detritus in the tank's substrate will have less to feed on and will not be so problematic in the tank. Replacing the debris-trapping media about two to three days after your moray feeds is a well-advised practice, for doing so will rid the ammonia-causing bio-debris as quickly as it accumulates in the filter.

When used in conjunction with one another, the benefits of biological, chemical, and mechanical filtration are amplified into a working system that keeps your aquarium water as clean, healthy, and sparkling clear as possible. By biologically transforming, chemically processing, and mechanically removing organic wastes from the water column, you can establish in your tank a high degree of filtration and purification much akin to that which your moray would enjoy in nature.

Protein Skimming

For those of you not familiar with the concept of protein skimming the marine aquarium, here's a ten second crash course: Most undesirable (nitrogenous, organic, etc.) debris in the marine environment rises to the surface through natural gas-exchange processes and collects there. A protein skimmer is a device that capitalizes on these gaseous properties by bubbling a dense torrent of air inside a tube through which aquarium water passes. Dirty water goes in, sea-crud gets trapped in gaseous foam, clean water re-enters the tank, leaving behind the floating bits of bio-matter that is trapped in a cup at the top of the processing cylinder. Protein skimmers come in both internal and external varieties, and it is the external variety that works best for morays, as any internal items only complicate matters in the moray tank, possibly causing any number of problems.

Because of morays' excessive wastes (and sensitivity to those accumulated wastes), a moray tank will require a powerful protein skimmer; more so, the living reef will suffer under the moray's wastes sooner than the eel will. Select a skimmer with a high contact time of bubbles-to-surface, and one that generates very tiny air bubbles. This combination will trap even the smallest surface-scum particles (tiny bits of undigested scale, shell, and solid wastes). Skimmers with added ozone, while not suited for all aquariums, are excellent choices for any moray tank. As is true with all filter apparatus, make sure the gaps surrounding the intake and return hoses are too small for the eel to slither through.

Protein skimmers are a must-have for serious marine hobbyists wishing to provide the best water quality to their morays. Of course, that doesn't mean you can skimp out on the water changes!

Water Changes: The Holy Grail of Moray Husbandry

While all this filtration is a great thing, nothing can compare to the refreshing qualities of good water-change practices. In the wild, morays enjoy water changes with every turn of the tides, the old water of the reef ebbing back into the deep, and a new, fresh wave of water flowing in from the open ocean. In captivity, old tank water will become stale–regardless of filtration–and detrimental to your moray. Over time, the animal's colors will fade, its appetite may dwindle away, and its general level of activity will become depressed. In stale water, sea life may survive, but it will not *thrive*. By changing even 15 to 20 percent (25 to 30 percent in tanks with larger bio-loads) of the aquarium water weekly, you can breathe new life into the aquarium, refreshing and rejuvenating all the life contained therein. Because they stay at the bottom of the tank, morays are constantly subject to the worst conditions of the tank; the bio-load having accumulated in the substrate and the heaviest, hostile gases lingering just inches above the substrata.

Start by treating a bucket or two of freshwater with the appropriate amount of salt, pH buffer, etc. Test to make certain that the bucket water is of exactly the same chemical composition as your tank water, then siphon-off an equivalent amount of aquarium water to be disposed of. Gently pour the new water into the tank, and watch your aquarium come to life. It's wise to heighten the security during this procedure, as morays will likely stress during all this commotion in the tank, and may attempt escape. Move slowly and methodically, rather than suddenly and clumsily, to make this period as stress-free as possible for your moray. Schedule your water changes about two days after feeding to remove your moray's nitrogenous excrement as soon as it enters the water column.

Because morays are scaleless animals, they are particularly sensitive to compromised water conditions (second only to corals and delicate polyps in their positive reception of water changes). Water changes stimulate the animal's senses, promote healthy appetite, reduce stress levels, and boost the immune system and mucus coating dramatically. Regularly scheduled water changes in the moray tank can mean the difference in an animal that lives for 3 to 5 years, and one that lives for over 20 to 25 years.

Siphoning the Right Way

I include this section because I've known a great many hobbyists who have conducted one water change after another only to see ammonia levels rise and pH levels drop daily in their tank. Frustrated and at a loss for answers while their livestock continues to suffer, these hobbyists could have prevented all their problems by siphoning the correct way.

Ammonia and nitrites are large molecules that are perhaps the heaviest gases in the tank. For this reason, they sink to the bottom of the tank and accumulate there, making the lower levels of the tank far more polluted than the upper levels. Not to mention the fact that the detritus—the decaying organic matter—has settled deeply into the substrate. Therefore, siphoning water from the top of the tank will do minimal good. Extend the siphon into the depths of the tank, gently spearing the nozzle into the substrate. Notice just how much dark, rotting crud gets sucked up. Once the water again runs clear in the siphon, raise the nozzle, allow all substrate to drop back to the tank's floor, and spear the nozzle into a new spot, again sucking up large amounts of bio-waste. Be careful not to stir up excess debris, as any rotting debris drifting in the water column could get lodged in your moray's gills or nares, possibly causing severe infection.

Using hang-on filters will not only allow you to access your filter media easily, but the outflow from the filter will help aerate the water, too.

By siphoning up both the ammonia and the nitrogenous materials accumulated at the bottom of the tank *and* a huge amount of the organic matter responsible for those materials, you've just conducted one healthy water change, and your eel will thank you for it!

Oxygen and Aeration

Oxygen and adequate aeration are some of your greatest allies in the battle against ammonia. Since ammonia tends to settle in the bottom of the tank, its accumulation is extra hazardous to morays, as their bottom-dwelling habits place them directly in the line of fire should ammonia levels become problematic. Ammonia does its damage by replacing oxygen in the moray's blood stream: starving muscles and nerves of oxygen, and destroying the eel on the cellular level. Early symptoms may include the moray swimming and behaving as if it is drunk. This is understandable, since its brain is being robbed of much-needed oxygen. Curb ammonia spikes by supplying plenty of airstones deep within the tank. Long, rod-style or bar-style airstones placed along the back wall of the tank will help to break up the ammonia (the oxygen bubbles force the ammonia to the surface where it can dissipate) and add extra oxygen to the depths of the tank; thereby destroying the bad gases and augmenting the good ones in a single stroke.

High levels of oxygen are also beneficial to growth and muscular development, so adding extra aeration to the depths of the tank while your moray is young can make a dramatic difference in the rate at which it grows, as well as raising the upper limit of its (eventual) adult size. Eels living out their lives in oxygen-starved tanks are seldom as large, healthy, or as downright beautiful as ones raised with ample aeration.

6

Acquiring Your Moray

Well, here we are at long last. Your tank is up and running, the nitrogen cycle has planed off to livable levels, and all systems are a "go." Your tank is ready to receive your new moray eel. But *which* species is right for you? How do you know? Once you decide on a species, how do you go about picking the best individual eel? What are the signs of an unhealthy moray?

If you do not yet know which species of moray you want, read the Popular Species section of this book to determine which moray will thrive best under the care and marine aquarium conditions you can provide.

Conscientious Purchasing

Whatever source you obtain your moray from, be sure to inquire about the collection practices used in capturing the eels from the reef. Many collectors worldwide use potassium cyanide, sodium cyanide, or other such lethal chemicals to harvest fish and inverts from the reef. By squirting diluted amounts of these agents into holes within the reef, the collector renders the fishes unconscious, allowing him or her to simply grab the fish by hand, slip it into a collection bag, and move on to the next hole and squirt again. This is a malicious and short-sighted practice that leads to rampant destruction of the reef. Not only do 90% of cyanide-collected animals die within days of collection, but the cyanide itself kills the reef outright. Each time a cyanide collector squirts his lethal cocktail into the reef, hundreds of coral polyps and other micro-organisms are bathed in the poison and die, creating a dead spot within the reef. Over time, these dead spots become more

and more numerous until the entire reef ecosystem lies in ruin; a once Utopia of sea life becoming an underwater graveyard of dead coral and empty waters. While cyanide collecting is illegal in many areas, some poachers still practice it, and rely on unsuspecting hobbyist to keep their blood-market alive.

Make sure that the pet shop or online wholesaler from which you purchase only sells animals that were net-collected without the use of any chemical agent. Not only is net-collecting infinitely gentler on the reef and the specimen collected, but it is a legal, viable use of the reef-resource that ensures future generations will be able to enjoy the natural wonders of the reef both in the wild and in the marine aquarium. For more information about cyanide collection and what you can do to curb this malicious practice, I refer you to Robert M. Fenner's *The Conscientious Marine Aquarist*, T.F.H./Microcosm Professional Series. Read chapter 10, it's an excellent, eye-opening chapter that all hobbyists should read prior to entering the hobby.

Appearance

A healthy moray eel (regardless of species) should be a *boldly* colored animal. I say "boldly" instead of "brightly" because a great many morays are naturally dark, and it's hard to define a "brightly dark" animal. Greens should be rich and dark, blues should be electric, grays should look like imposing storm clouds, blacks should be like midnight, and whites should be as pure as snow. Rich, uniform coloration is the first visible sign of superior moray health. Avoid purchasing specimens with faded or "washed out" coloration. After viewing a few individuals of the same species (or even just looking at the pictures in this book), it will become clear what a healthy moray is supposed to look like. Faded colors may indicate excessive stress, improper mucus production, a depressed immune system, or other serious problem. Likewise, vividly colored animals sporting blotches or patches of discoloration should also be avoided, as these areas may be bruises caused during shipping, amebic infection, or a fungal infection.

Once you determine the animal's color is as it should be, look to its fins and the texture of its body. A healthy moray will have a continuous dorsal/caudal fin that begins just behind the head and runs to the underside of the tail. This fin should be free of nicks, scrapes, tears, holes, or other imperfections. Inflammation along the fin is also a definite red-flag, as such a lesion could indicate the onset of infection or mishandling in transit. Now check the rest of the body for any signs of trouble. The skin should be universally smooth and even. Any cuts, open sores, bruises, abscesses, or noticeable bumps on the skin are indicators that the animal's health

This is an excellent specimen of Snowflake Moray (*Echidna nebulosa*), which is a very popular and readily available species for the hobbyist to obtain.

is in question and is not fit for purchase. The eyes should be clear and have clean edges. Watch out for cloudy or puffy eyes, or those with excess mucus or film around the edges. Likewise the nares, mouth, gill openings, and anus should all be clean, clear, and functioning properly. Anything out of the ordinary in these areas is cause to start looking for another eel.

Lastly, check for external parasites. Anything "extra" clinging to the skin or fins of the moray is likely a parasite, and can cause more trouble than it's worth. Keep on searching. If you have special ordered the animal, have the pet shop keep it for a while longer until such symptoms heal or disappear. There is no reason to purchase a sickly animal simply because the shop cannot provide you with a quality one.

Behavior

If it has not been in the store a long time, a newly imported moray will likely exhibit an "extreme" behavior, either to the skittish and shy end of the spectrum, or it may be given to high levels of random, boisterous activity. Neither of these scenarios is cause for alarm if the eel has been imported within the last 48 hours, as it sometimes takes days for a moray to calm down and adapt to the sights and sounds of its new home. If either of these conditions continues, however, there may be problems.

Your new moray should be curious and willing to come out and investigate its new surroundings. Morays that hide all the time may have health problems and should be carefully observed.

Shyness is quite natural in most morays, as their retiring disposition will often draw them deeper into hiding when some eager hobbyist is pressing his or her face and fingers against the glass. Just as long as the shyness does not impede the moray's willingness to take food, everything is fine. A free-swimming, excessively active animal may just be a little nervous or rambunctious in the pet shop's tank, though it may also develop problems adapting to captive life. This behavior is most frequently seen in old adult specimens. Like many animals that are collected from the wild, some adult morays have a very hard time adapting to life in the aquarium. Purchasing such an animal is ill advised, as it is, in the home aquarium, prone to escape, injury, and violence within the tank, and violence against its keeper; making for a real heart-ache of an endeavor. A hobbyist's best safeguard against purchasing a non-adaptive specimen is to watch the animal feed in the pet shop's tank. When a moray is truly stressed or feels that its life is in peril, the last thing on its mind is food. If it will take a meal in captivity, it will soon settle down and live a normal life in your tank. Watching a prospective moray eat in the pet shop is a good idea under any circumstances, even if the moray looks healthy in all other ways.

Perhaps the most desirable quality in moray behavior is curiosity. A curious eel that comes to the glass to meet your stare or follow your finger is a hobbyist's best

choice. Curiosity indicates low levels of stress, a high degree of comfort in captivity, and healthy, fully-functioning senses. In the wild, many moray species are naturally curious, and the best specimens will remain that way in captivity. Curiosity is also a likely indicator of a benevolent disposition. A shy or overly active moray may be given to aggression in the aquarium, but an inquisitive specimen is typically gentle and slow to anger, making that specimen the best candidate for coexisting with a range of tank mates.

A truly graceful animal, a moray should have even, fluid movements about it when it breathes and swims. A healthy moray is the picture of elegance, while a sickly or dying one will move in quick, jerky motions. Unevenness, random twitching, and seemingly involuntary movements or muscle spasms are key indicators that either the aquarium conditions are poor (very high ammonia will cause such symptoms) or that the animal's nervous system has, for whatever reason, gone awry. In either case, do not purchase, as the moray may give up the ghost within a span of hours.

A healthy moray will always hold itself upright in the tank, keeping its belly to the substrate and its dorsal fin pointing roughly upward. An animal that stays tilted or slanted, or one that is completely upside-down is definite cause for alarm. Also known as "side-swimming," this seeming loss of equilibrium is usually an indicator

Morays should have even, fluid breathing motions. Those that don't may be suffering from exposure to poor water quality or parasitic infestations of their gills.

that something is seriously wrong with the animal, and death may be just over the horizon. Do not purchase such an animal under any circumstances! A moray should also hold its head up. A specimen whose head is down or allowed to rest perpetually on the substrata is likely quite sick. Almost all of a moray's sensory organs are located in its head, and a spry individual is always using these senses (sight, smell, and cranial-based lateral line) to monitor minute changes in its surroundings. So when the head is down or seems lifeless, the eel's senses are not functioning properly. The animal is suffering under serious ailment.

When it comes to breathing, a moray should breathe at a slow, regular, unhurried pace, the jaws rhythmically flexing up and down, forcing water over the gills in a definite and gentle manner. Avoid specimens with rapid or irregular breathing rates. A "gentle and paced" rate of breathing may not be easily determined at first glance, but after viewing a few morays, it will become clear which ones are breathing well, and which are breathing at rapid or greatly reduced rates.

Quarantining New Arrivals

As is true with all marine fishes, never introduce your moray directly into your display tank. Place it in a quarantine tank, which is maintained to the same chemical standard as the display tank, for three to four weeks. Anticipate a high level of stress and boisterous activity in your moray during its first few days in a new home. Jumping, vigorous swimming (perhaps with the head and snout out of the water), and repeated escape attempts are common and must be thwarted. If your moray does get out of its tank, pick it up off the floor with a wet towel or washcloth (as gently as possible), carefully rinse off any debris, and place it back into the quarantine tank. Increase aeration and pray for the best. Morays are survivors, and even the most dried-out, seemingly mummified specimens can be revived, almost magically resurrected, a few hours after being returned to their tank.

Acclimatize your moray to its new, albeit temporary, home slowly. Float the pet shop bag in the quarantine tank for about an hour to regulate temperatures, and pour about ½ cup of quarantine water into the pet shop bag every half hour, and add a small air stone to the bag. Repeat until at least three hours have passed. This way, not only will your new addition be fully adjusted to the temperature of its new home but it will be adjusted to the water chemistry of the quarantine aquarium as well. Release your new moray into quarantine. After the quarantine period is over, acclimatize your moray to the display tank by repeating this gradual process outlined above.

While in quarantine, your moray should only have inert (unreactive) tank décor in the tank with it. This will ensure that any medications that need to be used will not react to it and form dangerous compounds.

During the first few days of acclimation to both quarantine, and later to the display tank, I recommend leaving the aquarium lights on dim, or illuminating the tank only slightly with another light in the room. Turning on a nearby lamp, for example, will allow you to observe the events transpiring in the tank, but will not stress or expose the new moray. After two or three days, begin your regular lighting/feeding/cleaning regimen. Congratulations, dear hobbyist, you are now the proud owner of your very own moray eel. May both it and you share years of marine aquarium bliss!

7
Feeding Time

Every hobbyist, everywhere, under every circumstance loves feeding time in the moray tank. And why not? It is only when they are feeding that we can witness our moray eels doing what they do best: bearing their teeth, slashing at their prey, and devouring their food just as they would in nature. The golden rule of a moray diet is to never feed your eel seafood that has been treated with salt, food coloring, dyes, preservatives, or a host of other artificial agents which can prove fatal to your moray and any other fish which may consume these items. Always try to provide pet shop fare that is specifically designed for use in the home aquarium.

Feeding Schedules

Because morays can put on quite the display when feeding, we hobbyists tend to overfeed; either by feeding very large meals or by offering meals too frequently. In some instances, the zealous keeper will commit both of these marine blunders. Not only is overfeeding frightfully unhealthy for our morays—causing obesity and ultimately cutting short the animal's life—but the bio-waste produced by the moray can severely and quickly pollute the tank, causing spikes in ammonia/nitrites/ nitrates. Excess bio-waste equates to poorer water conditions for the moray and much more work on the part of the hobbyist in water changes, siphoning, and general maintenance. Digestion in morays is relatively slow, and while these animals will not often hesitate to feed if given the opportunity, food can back up in their throat, possibly causing bloating, irritation, inflammation, and even infection

within the upper digestive tract.

For these reasons alone, a strict feeding schedule should be established for any species of moray eel. Large morays will require large meals, but should be fed less frequently than their smaller cousins. Conversely, smaller morays need to eat more frequently, but favor smaller meals over a gut-swelling feast. A good schedule is to feed your moray once a week: feed an amount of food that is (in total mass) no more than about two times the size of the eel's head. For example, once a week, I'd feed a 20-inch Snowflake Moray 2 to 3 shrimp/squid/silversides/clams that were no bigger than the last joint of my thumb. A 20-inch Snowflake is an adult near the upper limit of its size, so seven days is plenty of time for it fully digest and metabolize this meal before offering more food. Smaller morays will require more frequent feedings of smaller food items, but be careful to not exceed three feedings per week. Older adults may not need to be fed more than once every ten days to two weeks. Adhering to this schedule will keep your moray as healthy as possible, while minimizing the bio-load in your tank and reducing required maintenance on your part.

But, of course, there are no hard and fast rules when it comes to feeding. At

While many morays will do well in the company of others, feeding time may be an exception. Make sure that enough food is offered to all parties involved, as weaker fishes may suffer from malnutrition over time.

higher temperatures, morays will metabolize their food faster, sooner. While my feeding schedule for a 20-inch Snowflake in may work just fine, the same dietary regimen in your tank, which is kept at /ɔ ɪ, might not be sufficient. Remember that as long as your moray is growing in *length*, it may require a little more food. But when it starts putting on more girth than length, you'll probably want to cut back on the frequency of meals.

A good way to take the guesswork out of all the nuances of all of this is to stick to a staggered schedule. The first week, feed your moray a small meal only once. The next week, offer a slightly larger meal, or offer two small meals about four days apart. This large-meal/small-meal rotation closely simulates how the eel would feed in nature (sometimes prey is abundant, sometimes it's scarce), and helps to promote a natural rate of growth.

A Moray's Diet: What's On the Table?

Easily the most important aspect of dietary concerns is the matter of variety. Variety of food items will either make or break your moray endeavor. Imagine you come home from work and sit down to a hamburger dinner. When you rise for breakfast, you reach into the refrigerator and grab another hamburger. Lunchtime rolls around, and you find yet another hamburger on your plate. It's not going to take long before you get tired of hamburgers. Then you'll get really tired of them, and before you know it, you're going to absolutely hate them. The very idea of eating another one of those beef, bun, and pickle concoctions just makes your stomach turn. The same is true of the moray eels. Feeding a moray the same thing, week after week after week will soon grow boring to the animal, then distasteful. Finally, the very food item that the eel once ate with relish will seem downright repulsive to it.

In the wild, morays will dine on just about anything they can get, and the variety of life on the reef guarantees that these predators will receive a wide range of foods. A damselfish here, a mantis shrimp there, and maybe a small squid for a midnight snack. Variety of food not only stimulates the eel's natural feeding instincts and curbs feeding-time malaise, but also affords the animal superior nutrition and vitamin intake. Feeding the same thing to excess will either starve a moray of much-needed nutrients, or offer it way too much of another nutrient, possibly leading to vitamin toxicity. Attain dietary balance by mixing it up. Feed cut up fish, mussel, clam, cockle, peeled shrimp, crabmeat, krill, mysis, prawn, octopus tentacles, silversides, etc.

Feeding your moray a varied selection of fresh seafoods is a much better alternative to using live foods.

Of course, not all morays will sit idly by while you feed only one type of food. If it feels the need for more nutrition than what you offer, a hungry moray is much more likely to attack and consume its tankmates, while a moray thriving on a varied and balanced diet will not be so quick to eat its companions. In fact, a great many hobbyists complain of their moray refusing to eat offered food, but preys relentlessly on its tankmates. This is the animal's way of obtaining the nutrients it needs for proper dietary health. Nature will play by nature's rules, and offering a variety of natural fare is the best way to keep your moray healthy, happy, and nonpredatory within the community tank.

Live vs. Cut Fare

I've known many hobbyists over the years who have fed live fare to their morays. The keeper watches intently as the moray exercises its hunting instincts of sniffing out the prey, tracking it down, and slaughtering it utterly. While this is at once a brutally engrossing and true-to-life behavior, it is detrimental in the home aquarium for two reasons. First of all, there is a lot to each prey item that the moray will not eat. A milky cloud of bodily fluids, antennas, scales, fins, legs, tails, and bits of shell are the side effect of feeding live foods, and these discarded items

can *seriously* pollute the water column. Morays produce enough bio-waste as it is, but allowing such uneaten tidbits to remain in the tank will rapidly lead to a lethally low pH and dangerously high levels of ammonia and nitrogenous buildup. Cut or frozen food offers as much or more nutrition as does live, and produces only a fraction of uneaten scraps left to rot in the water.

Secondly, feeding live food promotes the eel's predatory nature that it may come to act just as it would in the wild: viewing every moving thing as potential food. Most captive moray bites are the result of an anxious moray lashing out for the shrimp-like fingers of its keeper. Feeding pre-killed or cut foods and presenting them to the moray on a regular schedule will help to condition it into only accepting food in that manner. Morays that are live fed are also much more prone to fight with or consume tankmates. The only exception to this rule is the Ribbon Moray, which thrives on a very specialized diet of live mollies, and might sooner starve than accept cut foods.

Never feed cooked, steamed, blanched, or otherwise processed foods to your moray. Cooking removes many of the beneficial nutrients from the food, and, while your moray may eat seemingly healthy amounts of food, the nutritional value of

Feeding morays live fishes promotes the eel's predatory nature. However, they may begin to eye up everything that moves as a potential meal.

each meal is so low that your eel may in fact be slowly starving to death. Offer only raw, unprocessed foods.

Feeding Methods

Let's speak now about the proper ways of feeding a moray eel. Morays have very poor eyesight and may have a hard time zeroing in on their food. In a community tank, this can present a real problem, for if you simply drop the food into the tank and rely on the eel to find it, any fast, visual hunters, such as lions, puffers, or groupers will certainly get to the food before the eel does. Instead, impale the food on the tip of a long, plastic skewer, and position it directly in front of the eel. If the moray is hungry, it will not hesitate to snatch the food from the skewer. (Holding the food in a pair of long feeding-tongs often works equally well.) Feeding the tank's faster inhabitants before you feed the eel is also a good idea, for once they have a full stomach, these fish will be less likely to come for the eel's food.

Hand-Feeding

Don't do it. Hand-feeding is an interesting and intimate practice through which some hobbyists feel they get closer to their pets. Hand-feeding allows the hobbyist to truly interact with his or her moray, and I'm sure that all your friends and family will be utterly amazed to see your Dragon Moray taking cut hunks of squid from your fingers. Let me assure that, "Hey, man, watch this," can quickly turn into, "Hey, man, I need some stitches!" Because of their poor eyesight, morays cannot readily distinguish where the food item ends and the fingers begin, and risking serious injury just to hand-feed your moray is not advised. Even dull-toothed, benevolent species such as the Snowflake or Zebra Moray can accidentally inflict painful wounds.

Vitamin Supplements

Supplementing your moray's diet with a broad-spectrum vitamin is always a good idea. Vitamins boost the animal's immune system, enhance its color and protective slime coating, stimulate a healthy appetite, and help to balance protein absorption and metabolic processes.

Younger, faster growing morays need more vitamin supplements than do mature individuals, and not all vitamins should be given in the same amount. Calcium, for example, if given to excess will pass through the eel's system with no problems, while vitamin A may accumulate in the animal's body until it reaches dangerous

Soaking food items in a highly palatable vitamin supplement will greatly benefit your moray eel's health in the future. Of course, be sure not to overdo it.

levels of toxicity. Fortunately, morays have a very hardy constitution and, under normal circumstances, are not prone to suffer from vitamin toxicity. Supplement by thawing the morays' food and placing it in a shallow dish of liquid vitamins for one to two hours prior to feeding. The vitamins will permeate the food item and coat the outside, so that when fed, the moray takes in a healthy dose of the good stuff.

I remember a time when a vitamin supplement regimen looked something like a mad scientist's lab: bottles and liquids of all types, mixing spatulas and glass test tubes containing the strangest concoctions of powders and potions imaginable. Advancements within the hobby have come a long way since then, and most commercial multivitamins are specifically balanced to promote good health among aquarium fish, and every species of moray can benefit from the same multivitamin. Soaking food items in a vitamin supplement is far preferred over adding vitamin supplements directly into the water column (which will nourish microorganisms and algal blooms, but probably not your moray).

8

Diseases & Disorders

"**R**esilient to disease, sensitive to medication." This truism of moray husbandry is another of those golden rules that can be critical to a successful moray venture. Moray eels are extremely hardy animals when housed in stable, clean environments. They are particularly sensitive, however, to chemical pollutants and fluctuations in water quality. When stressed by such conditions, a moray—any species of moray—can easily weaken and take ill. Fortunately, most of these disorders are easily treated and if caught quickly, are seldom fatal. Because of their stalwart constitution, most morays will fully recover and bounce back from just about any of the following maladies.

External Parasites

There are a whole host of external parasites that may afflict a moray eel: hookworms, leeches, protozoa, flatworms, etc. Despite their variety in form, however, these vampiric invaders have one common goal in mind: drink blood. External parasites normally cannot bore through a moray's slime coat, but stressed or sickly individuals having a reduced mucus shield are prone to parasitic attacks. Whether by their needlelike rostrums, rasping tongues, or dagger-sharp teeth, each parasite will anchor itself to its host moray and bore into the flesh, tapping a capillary for the precious red fluid. Once the parasite has taken its fill of blood, it will drop off, mate, lay eggs asexually, or simply divide on the cellular level, depending on species. Whatever the case, one parasite ultimately can become thousands over a very short amount of time, and until the cycle is broken, these

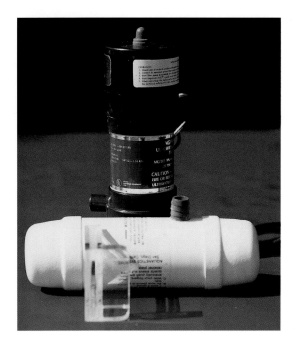

Incorporating an ultraviolet sterilizer into your system will greatly reduce the number of potentially dangerous parasites that your moray could become exposed to.

blood-sucking invaders will tap your moray for all it's worth.

Fortunately, external parasites are perhaps the most easily recognizable and curable of all ailments; losing a moray to external parasites is a rare occurrence in the tank of a conscientious hobbyist. A moray suffering from a parasitic attack will typically exhibit loss of appetite, listless behavior, and endless scratching (flashing) against sand, substrate, rocks, coral or whatever is nearby in order to rid itself of the attached parasites. Of course, the most obvious sign of infestation is the parasites themselves: tiny dark or whitish spots, blotches, or worms adhering to the skin. Density is usually greatest near the moray's head, throat, and gills, as these areas receive the highest amount of blood flow.

Once the presence of a parasite is confirmed, remove the moray from the display tank and perform a 10 to 12 minute freshwater dip. Since all external marine parasites buckle under freshwater like a vampire in the tropical sun, a huge percentage of them should fall off during this dip, at which time an exact identification, with the aid of a magnifying glass, is usually possible. Severe infections may require two dips to be performed a couple of days apart. From there, move the moray to a quarantine tank dosed with 1 drop per gallon of 37 percent molar concentration (about 200ppm) of Formalin. Conduct thorough water changes (to the tune of 40-60%) daily for the next week to ten days in the quarantine tank and display tank

to break the parasite's cycle of life. Leave the afflicted moray in quarantine for at least 3 to 4 weeks to observe for further outbreaks. You may wish to conduct an extra week's worth of (50-60%) water changes in the display tank, making sure to siphon the substrate, thereby breaking the parasite's life cycle and ridding your tank of any unhatched or unattached parasites. Never use chemical treatments in a reef tank, and use care when treating in a fish-only tank. If you house only your moray in the display tank, treatment with Formalin is possible.

White Spot Disease

White Spot disease, also known as "Ick," is one of the most common marine maladies, and is easily diagnosed and treated. Appearing as a dusting of salt granules all over the moray's body, Ick is actually a type of parasite called a ciliated protozoan. These single-celled attackers attach to the eel's skin, suck minute amounts of blood, and drop off into the substrate. There they encapsulate, divide into hundreds of new cells, and hatch into a host of baby Ick. One encapsulated Ick cell may divide into a thousand new parasites.

Morays are highly resilient to Ick, and rarely contract it in the wild, though when housed in a tank in which an outbreak occurs, any species of moray may be beset by the parasite, which concentrates in close quarters. Begin by removing your moray from the display tank to a quarantine tank dosed with 1 drop per gallon of Formalin in strengths of 38 to 42 percent, making sure to remove any activated carbon for the duration of the treatment. Severe infections can be combated by conducting a freshwater dip. Since the marine Ick cannot live in freshwater, the bulk of them will drop off and die during the dip. The open sores left by the Ick on the moray's skin are highly sensitive and subject to secondary infection. Maintain supreme water conditions in the quarantine tank, and conduct water changes (about 50-60%) daily. Because the Ick have robbed your moray of its precious blood, increased feedings will strengthen the immune and metabolic systems, while a dramatic increase in aeration will compensate for the loss of oxygen-carrying red blood cells and afford your moray the all the oxygen it needs. This will lower the animal's breathing rate and ease its stress level. Under these hospitable conditions, the moray will soon regenerate its lost blood and the lesions should heal quickly. Leave the afflicted moray in quarantine for approximately 3 to 4 weeks.

To rid the display tank of Ick, conduct 50 to 75 percent water changes daily for eight to ten days to break the Ick's life cycle, making sure to siphon the substrate thoroughly with each cleaning, but *do not* treat the display tank if it contains a

calcareous substrate. Wash all nonliving tank apparatus in *very hot* water: nonliving rocks, nets, heaters, filter intake stems, filter media or foam inserts, etc. It is a guarantee that the Ick will have permeated these items, but since they disintegrate at temperatures above 90°F, they are easily eliminated. Most Ick infections can be prevented by thoroughly quarantining all new arrivals for at least three weeks prior to introducing them into the display tank.

Internal Parasites

Internal parasites are quite rare in moray eels, though they do exist. The hodgepodge of internal offenders includes cestodes, nematodes, acanthocephalans, and various protozoa. Exact identification may require an expert's examination of the moray's stool or blood sample. Symptoms range from loss of appetite, sharply increased appetite (often accompanied by mysterious weight loss, as the parasites metabolize more nutrients than does the eel), exaggerated breathing, loss of color—and in severe cases—visible parasites extruding from the mouth, nares, and anus. In the case of nematodes, free-swimming parasites may be visible in the water column as they search for a new host; these will appear as tiny, white, whip-like worms jerking and swimming in whipping motions throughout the tank.

Internal parasites can become very harmful if allowed to proliferate. One way to tell if your moray is infected is if it eats but loses or fails to gain weight.

Most of these parasites can be treated quickly and effectively with such medications as Fenbendazole, Piperazine, or Metronidazole. Remove the afflicted moray to quarantine, and treat the water with appropriate dosages (will vary depending on the exact medication). Remove all activated carbon and chemical filtering agents, as these items will absorb the medicine before it has a chance to cure your moray. Increase aeration in quarantine to boost oxygen levels in the eel's blood and to help expel nitrogenous gases from the tank. Increased feeding is also important during an internal parasite infestation, as the moray will need all the nourishment it can get to boost its immune system and protective mucus coating to ward off secondary (bacterial or fungal) infections. In some cases, with the guidance of a veterinarian, you may wish to feed your infected moray with medicated foods. Often, standard medications can be used in this technique but their doses are variable. This is why it's best to consult an animal health professional who specializes in the treatment of fishes for such cases. Of course, whenever treating infected fishes, be sure to maintain the highest water quality standards in the quarantine tank. Periodic blood or stool smears will confirm the presence or absence of internal parasites. The afflicted moray should remain in quarantine for 3 to 4 weeks, or longer if necessary until all traces of the parasite disappear.

Bruises, Lesions, & Other Injuries

Injuries are the number one ailment of moray eels in captivity, and range from mild facial abrasions from nosing around in small quarters, to serious cuts and deep-tissue bruises resulting from injuries obtained during escape attempts. Even when a large cut heals with no complications, it will usually leave a permanent scar, while the worst-case scenario can result in an open, festering wound that is slow to heal and prone to infection. Once an infection sets in, even a small, seemingly insignificant cut can prove fatal—particularly in the more delicate species such as Ribbon and Jewel Morays.

We certainly cannot predict that fateful instant when, as we open the lid to feed our tank, an overzealous moray rockets to the top, breaks the surface, vaults over the lip of the tank, and crashes to the floor below. However, we can construct our tank in such a way as to thwart most escape attempts and injurious situations. Secure your tank with a heavy lid that will not break if thrashed from beneath by a rambunctious moray. Likewise, take special care when cleaning the tank. Make no sudden moves or gestures that could frighten your moray. I've seen startled eels inflict serious damage to themselves by crashing headlong into the wall or lid of the tank while fleeing the handwc of their keeper.

Hazards within the tank include exceedingly sharp furnishings such as cracked or broken filter intake stems, jagged, dead corals, or even lava rock, which is a great substrate for cultivating nitrifying bacteria, but is perhaps the most abrasive substance on the planet. When housed in too small a tank or during its nightly exploration of its underwater world, a moray is prone to rub, nudge, bump, and scrape its head and snout against most things it encounters. As soon as such blemishes are spotted, try to determine what feature within the tank is the culprit and remedy the situation (by removing the offending item) before the wound can develop into something more serious.

If your moray is rubbing against everything in the tank out of curiosity, it may actually be looking for more adequate shelter. Morays suffering from too few hideaways are prone to rub their noses raw trying to burrow deeper into a retreat. Supply your moray with larger, deeper hideaways to satisfy its need for shelter and curb this self-destructive burrowing.

In nature, morays obtain food through their curious-by-instinct behavior: nosing in and out of caves and crevasses in search of resident crustaceans and sleeping

The Ribbon Moray (*Rhinomuraena quaesita*) needs a deep, soft substrate to prevent its skin from being scraped up. Such scrapes may lead to a potentially life-threatening infection.

fish. If this rubbing stems from the animal exercising its natural hunting instincts, increase its weekly food rations, as an inquisitive eel is less likely to go nosing around for prey if it has a full belly.

Some tankmates are the cause of heinous lesions and wounds, as well. Large, powerful crustaceans, triggers, angels, and large groupers can inflict wounds when engaging the eel directly, and smaller fish—when consumed by the moray—can do damage to their head, mouth, and throat, perhaps by holding erect the rays of its dorsal fin when being eaten by the moray, thereby inflicting puncture wounds inside the throat.

Whatever the cause of the injury, the treatment is largely universal. Remove the offending animal from the tank, place the moray in a quarantine tank with superior water quality, and simply monitor your pet for signs of infection. When the wound heals completely, return the moray to the display tank. If the wound contracts infection, treat with an appropriate antibacterial or antifungal medicine. Erythromycin is an excellent, wide-spectrum antibiotic, while a Furan-based medication can conquer most fungal attacks.

Fungal & Bacterial Infections

Fungal and bacterial infections almost never strike on their own. Rather, they most commonly are the secondary infections of a previous injury or trauma. Like vultures descending on a crippled animal, these insidious attackers move swiftly and bring certain death if left untreated.

Often brought into being by degraded water conditions, bacterial and fungal infections are identified as sores, patches of rough skin, bloody or recessed patches over which no mucus will form, or surface hemorrhaging along the skin and fins. Fungal infections also manifest as patches of rot or discoloration on the skin, or general milky film over the animal's body. If left in the tank, the infected moray will stress, depress its activity, and will almost certainly come under the attacks of its tankmates. Fish know when one of their own is weakened and vulnerable, and will try to make a meal of your ill moray one mouthful at a time. By nipping hunks out of the fins and flanks of the moray, your other marine fish can seriously worsen a bacterial or fungal infection.

These afflictions are best combated by removing the moray to quarantine, offering it superior water quality, and treating the water with proper dosages of either Erythromycin (for bacteria) or Furan (for fungi). If the infection is going to respond to the chemical treatment, you will see signs of recovery (increased

appetite, regaining of color, increased activity) within 24 to 36 hours. If nothing occurs during this time period, switch to a different medication. Treat until all the antibiotic is used up (to prevent a relapse), and keep the moray in quarantine until its wounds have healed, then return it to the display tank only after making drastic improvements in water quality.

Malnutrition & Vitamin Deficiency

Although not really a disease, malnutrition is one of the leading causes of death among morays in captivity. Fortunately, it is a malady that is easily corrected. Malnutrition typically comes from a lack of variety in the diet. Morays that are exclusively fed a diet of shrimp or cut fish often become listless and refuse to eat for extended periods of time. Nightly activity may reduce dramatically and the moray will begin to loose weight. Colors will likely fade, and the moray may spend much more time in hiding. Solve the problem by offering a wide variety of fare: shrimp, fish, prawn, squid, clam, mussel, crayfish, mysis, krill, oyster, etc.

Some hobbyists have made the mistake of cooking or blanching the food they offer to their eels. This practice robs the food of its nutritional value and will almost certainly lead to malnutrition and eventually starvation. Aside from thawing any

This very young Snowflake Moray (*Echidna nebulosa*) will need to be fed frequently on a high-quality diet rich in vitamins if expected to grow normally.

frozen food items or adding vitamin supplements, do not alter them: do not cook, season, or change their natural consistency in any way whatsoever.

A deficiency of vitamins can inhibit long-term growth and may lead to serious health problems. Symptoms of vitamin deficiency include: listlessness, fading of coloration, slowed breathing, lack of appetite, and in very young specimens, stunted or malformed growth, especially in the head and jaws. Slowed metabolic processes, inadequate mucus coating, and a very poor immune system also manifest from a deficiency in necessary vitamins. Morays that shed excessive amounts of mucus, or those whose mucus coating has all but worn off are particularly prone to contract other ailments and secondary bacterial and fungal infections. Remedy by soaking each food item in a broad-spectrum vitamin supplement designed for the marine aquarium.

Slime Shedding

Although not a disease in and of itself, slime shedding is often a sign that something is amiss in the tank. Similar to a canary in the coal mine, slime shedding is a symptom of a larger problem and may indicate a vitamin deficiency, poor nutrition, inordinate levels of stress, improper pH, or spikes in ammonia. Some

Power-Feeding

In an attempt to make their pet grow at an inordinately fast rate and to monstrous proportions, some hobbyists practice overfeeding, or "power-feeding." Offering copious amounts of food at excessively frequent intervals will make the animal grow very quickly, especially if power-feeding begins when the eel is very young and is naturally in a period of rapid growth. While power-feeding does cause rampant growth in the musculature and skeleton of the moray, it cannot increase the developmental rate of the internal organs and brain. The end result is a very large bodied, yet frightfully unhealthy specimen that is ultimately doomed to a short life. Numerous health problems will ensue, and a moray that could naturally live for two to three decades in captivity, may expire after as few as five years. Power-feeding is a cruel, shortsighted practice that is, unfortunately, irreversible. A conscientious hobbyist would never practice power-feeding, nor would he or she ever purchase an animal that is known to have been power-fed by a previous keeper. Signs of a power-fed animal include an insatiable appetite and an inordinately small skull and jaws.

...dding is normal, for as new slime is produced daily, the older ...yers are sloughed as thin strands extending down from the body. Often looking like tiny worms attached to the body, these strands will drop off after a couple of days, while a worm would stay attached. Normal, healthy amounts of slime shedding can be aided by adding a Scarlet Cleaner Shrimp *(Lysmata debelius)*, which will live in symbiosis with most morays, picking off and devouring the unsightly strands of sloughing mucus.

Severe mucus shedding (or the failure to produce any new mucus) can result in large patches of exposed, discolored skin. Mucus is the moray's first line of defense against ailments, and, once it falters, the moray is largely defenseless against bacterial and fungal infections as well as external parasites. The solution to excessive mucus shedding is to search for and correct the cause of the shedding. Have your water tested by a professional or pet shop dealer. Remove any tankmates that might be pestering your moray, improve water quality, balance the pH, and supplement or vary the diet you offer your moray. The most common cause of mucus shedding is adverse water conditions. In order to protect its skin from acidic or otherwise hostile water conditions, a moray will produce copious amounts of mucus daily, the older layers continually falling off to reveal fresh layers beneath.

Obesity

Obesity differs from power-feeding in that the hobbyist may not understand or recognize that their animal is overweight. Obesity in moray eels has much the same effect as obesity in humans and most other animals, and often cuts the animal's life short by several years. Obesity is recognizable by increased breathing rates, slow movements, and lack of muscular definition within the animal's flanks. Obesity is particularly prevalent among morays kept in cramped quarters where they have no room to swim about and flex their muscles as they would in nature. An obese moray may sport a plump or rounded appearance, while a normal individual of the same species will be sleeker and laterally compressed. A healthy moray should be able to coil itself tightly and move through even the narrowest of gaps. An obese moray will lose some of its powers of mobility; it may have trouble turning around inside its hideaway or may no longer coil into a small cave. Seriously obese animals may spend much of their time in the open, and will not swim nearly as vigorously as a healthy moray. Combat obesity by reducing both the amount of food offered and the frequency of the feedings.

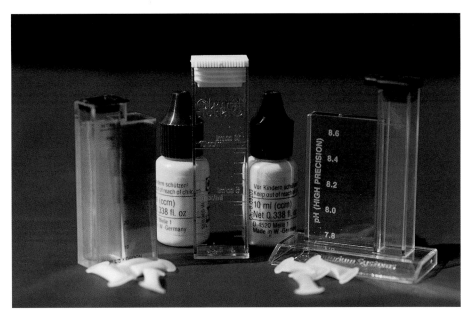

Performing water tests on a regular basis will allow you to keep a careful watch on your water's quality. As the water quality decreases, perform regular partial water changes.

pH Shock

Perhaps the most fast acting of ailments, pH shock occurs when the pH balance of the tank is thrown off, probably from adding improper water when conducting a water change, or the accumulation of bio-wastes, which can radically raise the acidity of the tank and lower the pH to lethal levels. A pH swing of even two or three tenths of a point can prove fatal to some of the most demure moray species, and can seriously stress even the hardiest of morays. Symptoms of pH shock include rapid breathing, loss of color, jerky and irregular movements, or upside down swimming. Your moray may behave as if it has been drugged, and, for all intents and purposes, it has been, for the chemical balance of its world has changed drastically, and its bodily systems are in shock.

While pH shock is often fatal, it is easily prevented by checking the pH daily and by conducting thorough, regularly scheduled water changes. If pH shock does occur, correct at once by conducting a water change and/or buffering the tank with a pH stabilizer and monitoring the eel closely. Recovery should be swift once the pH has returned to acceptable levels, but the stressed eels are not likely to feed or return to normal behavior for a few days or even a week, as they will not soon forget the trauma of a severe pH shock.

Nitrogenous Poisoning

Nitrogenous poisoning occurs when ammonia, nitrites, and nitrates are allowed to run riot in your tank. Feces, urine, dropped food (often fed to excess), and other decomposing organic matter in the tank can essentially turn the water into an unlivable vat of harmful gases and corrosive acids. Early symptoms include accelerated or erratic breathing (the moray is trying to increase oxygen to its muscles and regulate bodily functions), jerking or twitching motions, excessive mucus production, open sores along the head, flanks, and fins, and continual movements in the top levels of the tank (to escape the more heavily polluted depths).

Much like pH shock, nitrogenous poisoning is easily prevented by conducting regular, thorough water changes. Fortunately, the cure is attained through much the same formula. Move the afflicted animal to a quarantine tank of the highest water quality where it can be isolated from any tankmates. When suffering from nitrogenous poisoning, a moray's erratic behavior often attracts the attentions of its tank mates: other fish nip and bite at the dying eel as if they know it cannot defend itself. Triggers, angels, butterfly fish, and tangs are particularly known for this. In specimens with open sores, a week to ten days of antibacterial or antifungal treatment will be necessary to cure current or budding infections and ward off

The Fimbriated Moray (*Gymnothorax fimbriatus*), like all morays, is very sensitive to dissolved nitrogenous wastes in its aquarium.

potential infections. Feed the afflicted moray (with vitamin-enriched foods) as often as it will eat, and let it get plenty of rest while it heals.

Within the display tank, correct the offending water conditions at once, and do not return the moray until ammonia, nitrites and nitrates are absolutely zero, pH is 8.2 to 8.3, and temperature is stable at 74 to 79 degrees. Conduct weekly water changes (by siphoning the substrata) of 15 percent thereafter to prevent future bouts with nitrogenous buildup.

Tumors

Tumors are perhaps the most loathed of all moray ailments, for not only are they extremely difficult to diagnose, but they almost always end in fatality. Tumors may originate from various causes, ranging from internal scar tissue (maybe from an old wound) that grows, swells, and eventually puts pressure on the organs or nervous system, to a malignant growth under the skin that is very much akin to cancer in humans. Tumors growing near the surface are more easily recognized as raised, often discolored protuberances just under the skin, and may be surgically removed by a specialized veterinarian. Unfortunately, these subcutaneous tumors are the less dangerous of the two varieties. It is the deep-tissue tumors that are largely undetectable and inoperable, which present the most problems. Symptoms of a deep-tissue or malignant tumor are outlandish death throes: lashing of the tail, rapid or greatly reduced breathing, and general writhing in agony. These symptoms usually do not occur until a week before the moray is fated to die. Many hobbyists refer to deep-tissue tumors as the mystery disease, for symptoms of great discomfort are present in the last stages of the ailment, but no cure on the planet seems to help; the hobbyist remaining baffled until an autopsy reveals the presence of the growth.

If you suspect your animal has an inoperable tumor, you should consult several experts on the matter as quickly as possible, and, if there is truly nothing that can be done to save it, you can at least take mercy on your eel, offering it a quick, humane death. Net it out of the tank, put it in a large container filled with water, and put it into the freezer. Freezing simply slows the eel's bodily systems down until it falls into a deep sleep. Soon thereafter, the eel's heart stops. It is totally painless.

Moray Medications: The Last Line of Defense

In most cases, morays succumb to infection or illness because they were in a weakened state. Their immune system might have been down, mucus coating was subpar, or their stress levels were off the chart, thereby presenting the attacking agent with opportunity to gain foothold on an otherwise stalwart animal. Low-grade water conditions are typically the culprit, and by maintaining the highest standards in water quality, the hobbyist can prevent perhaps 99 percent of these ailments from ever taking hold. But if water quality does dip, and an infection of some type afflicts your moray, the first step, regardless of *what* ailment your eel has, is to check all parameters of water quality and improve them where needed. Many nonspecific maladies can be cured simply by upgrading your husbandry practices. These include: pH shock, nitrogenous poisoning, excessive slime shedding, obesity, and bruises and lesions. Superior water conditions also help the morays to help themselves, for only when under such high-quality water conditions are a moray's bodily systems most resilient and best able to fight off ailments.

When medication is absolutely necessary, it is best to follow the instructions on the bottle *verbatim* only when the product is designed specifically for morays. When using medicine designed for scaled fish species (as most medicine dosages are calculated based on scaled fish), use only half the recommended dosage, as this

Pay careful attention to water quality during periods of medicating. Many medications will kill off both good and bad bacteria, and this will lead to a buildup of ammonia and other pollutants.

medicine will have a much more potent effect on your moray (as well as any other scaleless fish you may have to treat).

Above all else: never, never, *NEVER* use non-chelated copper-based medications—neither on the eel directly, or in a tank that will ever house a moray. When exposed directly to copper medication, a moray is doomed to a most painful death: burning and writhing in the poisoned water. When housed in a previously treated and contaminated tank (the porous nature of calcareous substrate, rocks, shells, filters, and even the silicon bonding the tank's walls absorbs and retains high levels of copper), the fate is even worse—a long, protracted demise awaits your moray. By conducting numerous, thorough water changes (85-95%), you will normally rid your tank of residual copper and make it inhabitable by your moray.

Conducting a Freshwater Dip

When a moray is afflicted with an external parasite, conducting a freshwater dip is often recommended over risking an overdose on some medical potion. As the name suggests, a freshwater dip consists of removing your moray from the display tank, and placing it in a small (just long enough for the eel to stretch out) aquarium of freshwater. Buffer the water to the same pH as the display tank, and see that it is free of all heavy metals, such as copper, and chemical pollutants like iodide, fluoride, and chlorine—all of which are potentially hazardous to your moray. The only difference between the display tank water and the freshwater dip should be the absence of marine salt in the dip. Place the moray into the dip quickly, but gently, and have a strong, escape-proof lid at hand, for your moray *will* struggle. If left in this water too long, your moray would certainly perish, but a 10 to 12 minute bath (only 4-5 minutes for juveniles of any species) will not harm it. During this bath, any attached parasites will suffer greatly; the vast majority will drop off the moray's skin.

While no long-term damage is done to the moray during this procedure, the animal's body chemistry is temporarily thrown off balance and it stresses considerably. After the dip is over, leave the moray in the dark comfort of a healthy quarantine tank, and do not repeat the process for at least 36 hours. Used in conjunction with a competent medical regimen, a freshwater dip can be a curative godsend.

Part II

Popular Species

While there are nearly 200 species and subspecies of morays worldwide, only a scant few make it to the pet trade. Listed here are some of the most popular and most well understood of the morays you are likely to encounter. Each species has assigned to it a number 1 to 5 indicating their suitability in most aquariums that have been set up to house moray eels. In assigning these rankings, I have factored in the moray's hardiness, disposition, willingness to feed, maximum adult size, and general ability to thrive in captivity.

Suitability Index

1. Should only be kept in public aquaria, zoos, and by extremely advanced hobbyists associated with universities and other scientific institutions. This is either because of their monstrous size, delicate nature, or malevolent disposition. Most 1s are best left in the ocean.
2. These eels are a little tougher to manage than the 3s, and may not be as desirable as other species. Large and unattractive species are typically listed as 2s. Any casual or nonprofessional hobbyist is advised to steer clear of any moray with a rating less than 3.
3. These are marginal eels that the average hobbyist is advised against keeping. Owning a 3 is a bit of a gamble, but can be rewarding if kept by an advanced aquarist who can afford these animals the care and space they require.
4. Can be kept by beginners but require a little more experience or some slightly modified conditions in captivity if these eels are to thrive. Hobbyist's who have some previous moray experience will probably have very good success with an eel rated as a 4.
5. The best all-around specimens for keeping in aquariums, they are commonly docile, attractive, and manageable and are a hobbyist's best bet for success in the home aquarium. Furthermore, they are recommended to hobbyists of every experience level.

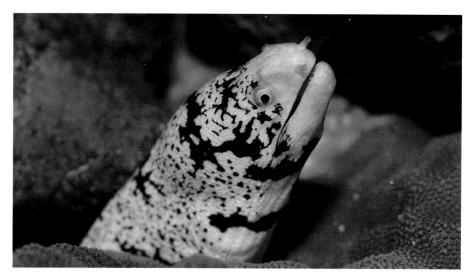

Echidna nebulosa / Snowflake Moray

Minimum Tank Size: 55 gallons.

Range: Found throughout the warm shallows of the Indo-Pacific region, Red Sea and Eastern Africa to the Society Islands and north through the Sea of Japan, east to Hawaii, Baja California, and from Costa Rica south along the coast of Columbia.

Size: 12 to 24 inches is common, over 36 inches is rare.

Natural Habitat: A shallow-water species, the Snowflake Eel frequents rocky outcroppings and coral reefs. Seldom living at depths below 30 meters, the Snowflake is also found amid intertidal reef flats, bays, lagoons, and throughout offshore reefs.

Diet & Feeding: Natural diet consists of a wide variety of crustaceans, mollusks, and small fishes. Captive diet should be as varied as possible with vitamin supplements accompanying every second to third feeding. Favored items include: live or cut shrimps, squid, cockle, mussel, and cut fish. One of the gentler morays, the Snowflake is renowned for taming, and taking food directly from the keeper's hands. This is a calculated risk, though the danger level is not critically high. I do not practice nor do I recommend the hand feeding of *any* species of moray.

Description: A slender eel, the Snowflake sports a low dorsal fin and rounded stature. The head is short with a blunt, rounded, and is accented with short nasal protuberances. Basecoat is alabaster white blotched in black to chocolate brown "snowflakes" that form loose bands or rings encircling the body. Bands may be interspersed with underlying yellow tint, especially around the head and neck. Space between the snowflakes is irregularly peppered in black to brown specks. Chin and nose are solid white. Eyes and nasal tubercles are bright yellow. Highly nocturnal.

Aquarium Suitability: 5.

Special Conditions: A master escape artist, the Snowflake Moray will likely find and slither through even the tiniest gaps in the lid of its tank. Because of its small stature, it can fit through holes that other species cannot. Adding a Snowflake Eel (or any other slender moray, for that matter) requires a serious re-evaluation of tank security.

Echidna polyzona / **Barred Moray**

Minimum Tank Size: 75 gallons.

Range: From the Red Sea and eastern Africa east to Hawaii. Also found at Ryukyu Islands and south to the Great Barrier Reef and throughout Micronesia.

Size: Large adults may near 30 inches, though 22 to 25 inches is average.

Natural Habitat: Reef flats, shallows lagoons, intertidal pools, and other areas of very clear, sheltered waters. Seldom ventures more than 10 to 12 meters down.

Diet & Feeding: Like most of its *Echidna* brethren, the Barred Moray is adept at feeding on crustaceans. Venturing out from its retreat, this animal will patrol the nooks and crannies of the reef in search of shrimps, crabs, octopuses, and recently molted lobsters. The Barred Moray is primarily nocturnal, though it may be active at all points of the clock.

Description: Wearing a base color of pale to charcoal gray or black with vertical bars of white to ivory or cream, the Barred Moray looks strikingly similar to its close cousin, the Zebra Moray, though the former's white bars are much wider. Head and lower jaw may be yellowish. Snout is short and rounded, and the teeth are peg-like and come to blunt points. When powered by this moray's strapping jaw musculature, these teeth are perfectly suited for crushing through the brittle exoskeletons of the moray's crustacean prey. Tail tapers noticeably to a distinct point, and dorsal fin is low.

Aquarium Suitability: 5.

Special Conditions: Barred Morays enjoy (and require) their caves and hideaways, but may move about the tank considerably more so than other (*Echidna*) morays. They must, therefore, be housed with tankmates that will not pester or stress them during the course of their daily roving. These animals do especially well when housed alone in a reef tank, though they can thrive with larger, benevolent fish species such as Lions or small groupers. Avoid mixing with fast moving or nippy species such as wrasses, tangs, angels, dwarf angels, and triggers.

Enchelycore pardalis / **Dragon Moray**

Minimum Tank Size: 125 gallons.

Range: Indo-Pacific. Hawaii to the Society Islands, north through the Sea of Japan and South Korea, south through northern Australia and New Caledonia.

Size: Captive specimens seldom exceed 30 to 33 inches, while wild individuals may reach 36 inches. Unconfirmed reports of 40-inch animals or longer are questionable.

Natural Habitat: Another dweller of the shallows, the Dragon Moray seldom ventures more than 50 meters down, as it is intolerant of deeper, colder waters. Frequents the living reef and its network of tight caves, overhangs, sunken wreckage, intertidal zones, and rocky coastlines.

Diet & Feeding: A devout piscivore, the Dragon Moray thrives on fish, though recently molted or delicate crustaceans are taken when the opportunity arises. Squid and octopus are particularly relished, and the ferocity with which a Dragon Moray will subdue these mollusks is not for the faint hearted.

Description: A stunningly gorgeous eel, the Dragon Moray is an absolute kaleidoscope of color. Although exact coloration varies greatly from one individual to the next, the base is typically brown to light cream or golden with white to yellow or golden spots and irregular blotches adorning the face and body, with vertical bars or contiguous blotches on the dorsal fin. Blotches may be outlined in gold. The exaggerated curvature of the snout and pronounced teeth identify this species as highly adapted to hunting fish; the jaws and teeth function to pierce the scales not of sleeping fare, but of active, struggling prey. Nares are exaggeratedly pronounced. Posterior nostrils accented by extremely long tubercles, which are situated directly over the eyes, giving the animal a distinct dragon-like appearance.

Aquarium Suitability: 4.

Special Conditions: The top causes of Dragon Moray mortality in captivity are poor water conditions and stress. Utilize superior filtration and protein skimming, and provide excessive shelter for your eel. During the acclimation process, this moray may spend 100 percent of its time hidden within the rockwork of the tank. Do not disturb it! This period of hiding is critical to its stress and health level, and as soon as it grows accustomed to the sights and smells of its new home, your Dragon Moray will emerge on its own. It does better in a quiet reef tank than in a fish-only tank, as the organic wastes produced by fishes can be problematic.

Gymnomuraena zebra / Zebra Moray

Minimum Tank Size: 75 gallons.

Range: Indo-Pacific. Found from the Red Sea and eastern coast of Africa, east to Hawaii and Ryukyu, south through the Great Barrier Reef.

Size: Average adult size is 30 to 36 inches, I have personally seen one specimen measuring 58½ inches, and have heard of individuals even longer than that, though Zebras of such proportions are exceedingly rare in captivity.

Natural Habitat: Another lover of the shallows, the Zebra Moray is a reef-centric species that seldom ventures far from to safety of the coral caverns and reef overhangs. Any dark, hidden retreat within its range is liable to house a Zebra Moray.

Diet & Feeding: With short, pebble-like teeth and powerful, stocky jaws, the Zebra can crack through the hard shells of its favorite foods: crabs, mollusks, snails, clams and other bivalves, and sea urchins. This moray is a slow moving hunter and mostly forages along the sea floor in search of shelled quarry. Seldom eats fish.

Description: True to its common name, the Zebra Moray sports a stunning coat of gray to black or purple to maroon striped with solid or broken vertical bars of white to cream or yellow. Head is short with a blunt snout and reddish eyes. Nares are highly reduced in this species, though its sense of smell is quite acute. A heavy-bodied eel, the Zebra Moray has a rounded frame, typical of the slower moving species.

Aquarium Suitability: 5.

Special Conditions: Not a reef-safe animal. Only corals and anemones will thrive in the company of a Zebra Moray. All crustaceans, mollusks, bivalves, and echinoderms are potential prey items. In the fish-only tank, provide this eel with at least four inches of substrata and plenty of structure for security. Use caution when mixing with fish. While docile by nature, this moray may become mildly aggressive or nippy when food is present. The Zebra Moray is also prone to periods of aestivation, and may not eat or show itself for several weeks. This is no cause for alarm.

Gymnothorax eurostus / **Abbott's Moray**

Minimum Tank Size: 75 gallons.

Range: Indo-Pacific. Reported from Seychelles to Costa Rica, Panama, and Easter Island.

Size: May exceed 30 inches, though captive specimens normally max out at 24 inches.

Natural Habitat: A strictly nocturnal species, the Abbott's Moray takes refuge from daylight in inshore reefs, sunken ship wreckage, undersea caverns, and other sheltered, yet shallow areas. Large individuals may live in surprisingly small crevasses within the reef.

Diet & Feeding: An indiscriminate carnivore, the Abbott's Moray preys upon the small and unwary things on the reef: fiddler crabs, shrimps, small or freshly molted lobsters, squids, octopuses, and any fish small enough (and slow enough) to be eaten. The animal's reclusive nature suggests it feeds primarily on crawling things and sluggish organisms of the reef, as it is not a particularly fast predator, nor does it often expose itself by hunting in open waters.

Description: A truly beautiful creature, the Abbott's Moray ranges from a regal purple to light brownish coloration, and is freckled in tiny golden to yellow-brown spots. Head is densely speckled, though the tail is only faintly peppered. Snout is slightly elongate, but ends abruptly in a squared-off chin. Eyes and nares closely set together, and the cleft of the mouth extends to behind the eye. Moderate dentition, vomerines present, but not nearly the same caliber as that of larger *Gymnothorax* species.

Aquarium Suitability: 3.

Special Conditions: The Abbott's Moray needs perhaps more rockwork and more retreats than any other species of moray. If it does not feel secure within its aquascape, it will likely refuse food for extended periods of time, stressing and possibly starving itself to death. Supply numerous caves and hideaways, and house alone or in the company of extremely docile fish species.

Gymnothorax favagineus / **Blackspotted Moray**

Minimum Tank Size: Over 200 gallons.

Range: Throughout the Indian Ocean and Indo-Pacific. Red Sea east to the Philippines and south through the Great Barrier Reef and surrounding Papua New Guinea. Northern range extends into the Sea of Japan.

Size: A true titan among the morays, this hefty species may reach lengths of up to 10 feet, and may weigh over fifty pounds.

Natural Habitat: A top predator of the reef environment, this eel is found wherever food abounds. Often encountered by divers along the reef and in the port windows of sunken ships, the Blackspotted Moray also frequents sheltered bays, lagoons, rocky shallows, intertidal flats, cavernous overhangs, and the root entanglements of brackish estuaries and river deltas.

Diet & Feeding: An accomplished hunter, the Blackspotted Moray moves about under the cloak of night, foraging for sleeping fish, all manner of crustaceans, and especially cephalopods, which may comprise more then 60 percent of its diet in the wild.

Description: One of the most attractive of all morays, the Blackspotted Moray sports a base color of white to yellowish, but is covered in thousands of irregular brown to black spots. Seldom overlapping, these spots are situated tightly enough to form a honeycomb or chain-link pattern over the entire body, a quality that has earned this eel the alternate moniker "Honeycomb Moray" (not to be confused with the true Honeycomb Moray (*Muraena melanotis*) of the Atlantic Ocean). The Blackspotted Moray has perhaps the sharpest and most pronounced dentition of all morays: a double row of razor teeth lining the upper jaw, a single row on the lower, and a palate full of long, sharp vomerine teeth.

Aquarium Suitability: 1.

Special Conditions: Like the Green and Giant Morays, this species lives in mutualism with cleaner wrasses and shrimps. House in the company of a White-Banded Cleaner Shrimp (*Lysmata amboinensis*), Scarlet Cleaner Shrimp (*L. debelius*), or a Cleaner Wrasse (*Labroides dimidiatus*). Shrimps are preferred for this purpose, as a hungry Blackspotted Moray will not hesitate to devour its symbiotic wrasse.

Gymnothorax fimbriatus / Fimbriated Moray

Minimum Tank Size: 75 gallons.

Range: Ubiquitous in the Indo-Pacific. From Madagascar and eastern coast of Africa, east to the Society Islands, south to Queensland, and north through the Sea of Japan.

Size: One of the smaller of the *Gymnothorax* morays, the Fimbriated seldom reaches lengths greater than 30 to 32 inches TL.

Natural Habitat: Typically reef associated. Marine environments include coral reefs, shipwrecks, tidal flats, seaward ledges and reef overhangs, mangrove tangles, rocky outcroppings, grassy sandbars, and sheltered areas. Also thrives in brackish deltas, inshore estuaries, and harbors.

Diet & Feeding: Small fishes and all variety of bite-sized crustaceans.

Description: An attractive, spotted species, the Fimbriated Moray wears a basecoat of light tan, to greenish-yellow and is accented with darker spots scattered randomly over the body. Some specimens have heavier or lighter speckling than others, or heavier mottling in one spot. Some spots overlap, making for a blotching effect. Spots are largest on young morays, and tend to diminish in size and frequency with age. The Fimbriated Moray favors tight hideaways, and spends much of its day with only its head exposed. Primarily nocturnal. Like all *Gymnothorax* species, the Fimbriated comes equipped with elongate, arching jaws and impressively sharp teeth.

Aquarium Suitability: 4.

Special Conditions: Fimbriated Morays tend to be picky eaters in captivity, and may stop feeding abruptly and seemingly for no reason. To combat this, lessen the duration of any lighted period the tank currently experiences; no more than 8 to 10 hours of light each day. Offering a variety of foods (squid, octopus tentacles, silversides, etc.) may also prompt your Fimbriated into resuming its former eating habits. Lastly, soak the food in a marine multivitamin supplement, as proper vitamins tend to raise the animal's metabolism and stimulate a healthy appetite.

Gymnothorax flavimarginatus / **Yellow-edged Moray**

Minimum Tank Size: From 300 to 500 gallons or more.

Range: Widespread throughout the Indo-Pacific region. From the Red Sea and coastal Africa east through Ryukyu and Hawaii. South to New Caledonia and throughout Micronesia. .

Size: Another titan of the morays, the Yellow-edged Moray may grow to an impressive, though rare, 96 inches long. Wild specimens commonly reach lengths of 78 to 80 inches, while captive individuals seldom exceed 72 inches. .

Natural Habitat: Favorite haunts include deep-water drop-offs, rocky or coral-laden flats, sheltered shorelines, seaweed and macro-algae beds, and seaward reefs. Occurs at a range of depths, from ankle-deep tidal pools to over 160 meters down. Found wherever prey abounds, and may establish long-lasting territories: an individual eel staying in the same area for decades.

Diet & Feeding: Yellow-edged Morays are particularly sensitive to the sounds and water-borne vibrations emanating from struggling or injured fish. This hunting strategy makes the Yellow-edged Moray a powerful opportunist, striking at any time, day or night, when food is in the area. Prey items include sleeping fish and cephalopods, with octopuses being particularly relished. Juveniles feed primarily on small fish, shrimps, and other bite-sized crustaceans.

Description: Base color is yellowish and densely mottled with black to brownish spots and speckles. Eyes are bright red, and the elongate snout and forehead is often a pale gray to lavender color. Tail is a faded version of the body color, often light yellow to olive green. Reduced nares. Juveniles of the species are typically bright yellow with dark blotches. Large vomerine teeth accent this moray's menacing dentition, while the head is heavily laden with strapping jaw muscles.

Aquarium Suitability: 1.

Special Conditions: The Yellow-edged Moray is a very hardy species that may live for nearly half a century under the right conditions. Very large quarters (500 plus gallons), clean water with superior circulation and protein skimming, and a varied diet of fish and cephalopods (supplemented with vitamins) are all it needs. Take great care when feeding or cleaning its tank, as this species homes in on and attacks anything that seems to be struggling in the water. The irregular, clumsy movements of a keeper's hands are seldom distinguishable from the thumping and struggling of an injured fish. Benefits greatly from cleaner wrasses and cleaner shrimps.

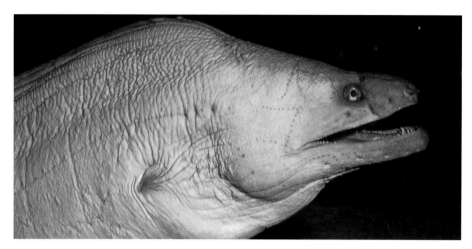

Gymnothorax funebris / **Green Moray**

Minimum Tank Size: 200+ gallons.

Range: Found throughout the western Atlantic from New Jersey south to Brazil and Ascension Island. Common throughout the warm, clear waters of the Florida Keys, Caribbean, and Bahamas. A singular specimen was found off Nova Scotia, Canada, though it is widely speculated that this individual was hopelessly lost, led astray by the Gulf Stream.

Size: 72 (average) to 96 inches TL.

Natural Habitat: Found in holes, crags, snags, and caves throughout the reef, the Green Moray's favorite haunts include reefs, tidal creeks, intertidal flats, lagoons, bays, grass flats, mangroves, and shipwrecks. A benthic species, the Green Moray also thrives in caves along the continental shelf and other shallow areas.

Diet & Feeding: Indiscriminate carnivores, the Green Morays, are, within their ecosystem, one of the top predators. While some morays employ a sit-and-wait strategy of ambushing passing prey, the Green Moray operates in a true hunter-killer mode. Common prey items include shrimp, crabs, lobsters, small fish, and especially squid and octopuses.

Description: A large, imposing species, the Green Moray is a stout-bodied creature. The tail is compressed laterally, making it a swift, powerful swimmer. The high dorsal fin adds to its fleet movements in the water. Like most members of the *Gymnothorax* genus, its head is stocky and robust, with a large mouth and sharp, well-developed dentition: dual rows of teeth on the forward upper jaw, a singular row on the lower, and a dual row of vomerine teeth in the palate. Taking its coloration and common name from its yellow-tinted mucus coating, the Green Moray's true flesh color is dark blue to black, hence the specific name *funebris* or "funereal." Nares are present, but relatively short. This animal hunts in total darkness, and locates prey with its keen sense of smell.

Aquarium Suitability: 2.

Special Conditions: Green Morays require very large quarters. I would never recommend housing even a small one in a tank less than 180 to 200 gallons; a tank over 400 gallons is optimal. Green Morays will thrive in commensalism with the Cleaner Wrasse *(Labroides dimidiatus)* or cleaner shrimp *(Lysmata* spp.), so dropping one or two in the tank is always a good idea. Greens thrive in either reef or fish-only tanks, provided its tankmates are not liable to end up on the menu.

Gymnothorax javanicus / **Giant Moray**

Minimum Tank Size: Over 1000 gallons.

Range: Throughout Indo-Pacific: Red Sea and eastern coast of Africa east to Micronesia and Oeno Atoll, north through Ryukyu and Hawaiian Islands, south to New Caledonia and Australia.

Size: HUGE! Large adult specimens may reach an astonishing 11 feet long and weigh as much as 75 or 80 pounds. Girth at its widest point may be equal to that of a man's thigh!

Natural Habitat: Found in lagoons, seaward reefs, reef overhangs, and especially in old ship wreckage at 0 to 50 meters deep. Steep slopes and offshore cliffs are also common haunts. Highly territorial. Once an individual establishes its range, it may well remain there for decades. Divers have reported seeing, and even naming, the same Giant Morays year after year in the exact same cave or sunken porthole.

Diet & Feeding: I like to think of the Giant Moray as the *Tyrannosaurus Rex* of the morays. With the exception of the sharks, this animal is far and away the dominant predator within its habitat, and virtually everything smaller than an automobile tire is on the menu: shrimps, crabs, lobsters, cephalopods, and all nonvenomous fishes. Surprisingly, only juvenile Giant Morays prey on crustaceans. Adults favor larger fare, for a shrimp to a Giant Moray is like a single kernel of corn or lone green pea sitting on our plate. It will not satisfy our hunger, and is too small to be trifled with!

Description: Base coloration ranges from tan to pale yellowish. Juveniles and sub-adults have numerous black spots over their entire body, while on inmature specimens, such leopard-like markings are isolated to the head, jaw, and gill areas. Jaws accented with heavy musculature. Juveniles are highly secretive, only moving at night, while adults brazenly swim about the reef in broad daylight. Body is extremely heavy and thick, though it is compressed laterally for speed in swimming.

Aquarium Suitability: 1.

Special Conditions: To be kept only by public aquaria. House in enormous tanks with only the largest of tankmates. Tankmates too small to be considered food are also suitable. The hobbyist or institution who can afford and manage it, can establish a stunning dichotomy of nature in a living reef tank with dozens of clowns, tangs, and other such small fish housed with a singular, massive Giant Moray. Always house with several cleaner wrasses or cleaner shrimps.

Gymnothorax meleagris / Turkey Moray

Minimum Tank Size: 200 gallons.

Range: Widespread throughout Indo-Pacific. Found from the Red Sea and coastal eastern Africa to Micronesia and Hawaii, north through Ryukyu and south to Lord Howe Island.

Size: Large adults may attain lengths of 48 inches, though 36 to 42 inches is the average.

Natural Habitat: Occurs in coral-rich environments: lagoons, seaward reefs, intertidal zones, and rock-strewn flats. Perhaps the most shallow-dwelling type of all the morays, this animal is frequently encountered in waters less than three feet deep.

Diet & Feeding: Active by day and night, the Turkey Moray employs a most unusual hunting strategy: foraging among exposed reefs during low tide. Slithering from one tidal pool to the next, this moray will briefly leave the water, crossing expanses of dry land, in its pursuit of prey items trapped in the tidal pools. Feeds primarily on fish, but will also take some crustaceans and cephalopods.

Description: A stunningly beautiful eel, the Turkey Moray wears a coat of jet-black to dark brown, and is speckled in innumerable spots of yellow to white. A close view of the skin looks amazing like stars in the night sky, a trait that has earned this eel the alternate common name "Midnight Moray." The inside of the mouth is alabaster white, and a vexed or agitated individual will hold its mouth wide agape, displaying this white color as a warning signal to "Stay back!" Should the offending animal approach further, the Turkey Moray will not hesitate to lash out, inflicting serious damage to its attacker.

Aquarium Suitability: 4.

Special Conditions: Because of its hunting strategy of leaving the water, this moray is highly prone to jump out of the tank. Take extra precautions in escape-proofing your aquarium when housing the Turkey Moray. Likewise, be alert at all times when opening or closing the lid, as a sudden, unexpected leap attempt by your eel is entirely possible.

Gymnothorax miliaris / Goldentail Moray

Minimum Tank Size: 100 gallons.

Range: Ever-present in the subtropical Atlantic. Found from southern Florida through the Caribbean and Bahamas south to the southern tip of Brazil and West Indies, and in the eastern Atlantic at Cape Verde, Ascension Island, St. Paul's Rocks, and the Isles of St. Helena. This moray can be found in the shallow waters surrounding almost all Atlantic islands.

Size: A laterally compressed species, the Goldentail grows to a modest two feet, with the occasional specimen reaching 30 inches TL.

Natural Habitat: A strictly reef-associated species, the Goldentail Moray thrives in warm, shallow waters that are teaming with life. Found amid corals, rocky shallows, grassy seabeds, mangrove tangles, and other sheltered shallows. Rarely does this species venture deeper than 50 to 60 meters down.

Diet & Feeding: Favored food items include all varieties of shrimps, as well as crabs, small or recently molted lobsters, or any bite-sized fish unfortunate enough to cross the eel's path.

Description: Typically sporting a base of dark brown to burnt umber, the Goldentail is peppered in yellow dots, the tiniest being on the head and neck, while larger dots freckle the body and tail. As its name suggests, the tip of the tail is pale yellow to a brazen or golden hue. The rare specimen has a reverse pattern: golden background peppered in irregular black dots. Such unusual animals always command a high price on the pet trade. Nasal nares pronounced, as is the posterior nostril. Sporting a relatively large head and laterally compressed body, the Goldentail is a quick, powerful swimmer and accomplished predator of the reef.

Aquarium Suitability: A definite 5!

Special Conditions: Because Goldentail Morays thrive in shallow, lively waters in nature, they benefit from well-lit conditions. Situate retreats so that the Goldentail can see most of what is going on in the tank around it. As the eel sits quietly in the mouth of its cave and watches the activity around it, it will feel more comfortable and will be more likely to behave exactly as it would in nature. Natural retreats, such as coral or live rocks, are preferred over artificial hides.

Gymnothorax mordax / **California Moray**

Minimum Tank Size: 150 gallons.

Range: Eastern Pacific, from Point Conception, California to southern Baja, Mexico, and westward to the Galapagos.

Size: Largest specimen on record is 60.8 inches long. Though 48 inches is average, with 50 or more inches not uncommon.

Natural Habitat: Favorite haunts include rocky reefs and stony shallows. Frequently encountered by divers in caves and holes, with only the head protruding. Not found at depths below 15 meters.

Diet & Feeding: A nocturnal hunter, the California Moray preys almost exclusively on crustaceans, with crabs being at the top of the menu. Shrimps and recently molted lobsters are also taken, as are unwary cephalopods. Hunting style is like that of the Green Moray: the California leaves its hole after sunset and patrols the nooks and crannies of the reef, nosing around and rooting out its prey.

Description: A stout-bodied animal, the California Moray wears a base color of greenish brown to solid brown, and may or may not be flecked in tiny speckles of yellowish green. Dorsal fin is moderately high, and nasal nares are present, but reduced. Head is large, and jaws are wide with musculature, alluding to this animal's powerful bite. Not overtly aggressive, but divers who have been bitten (sticking their hands blindly into crevasses in search of lobsters or abalone) report the California Moray to have a bulldog grip and general refusal to let go once attached. The only way to end such a foul scenario is to sever the animal's head. A tragedy, since most bites occurred through a diver's negligence, not the moray's aggression.

Aquarium Suitability: 3.

Special Conditions: Outfit a California Moray tank with lots of rockwork, for not only does it require daily retreats, but a California Moray's nightly wanderings keep it close to the safety and structure of the reef. Do not mix with motile crustaceans or fish under nine inches long.

Gymnothorax moringa / **Spotted Moray**

Minimum Tank Size: 400 gallons.

Range: Common along the eastern seaboard of the United States, Gulf of Mexico and throughout the Caribbean. Also found from North Carolina south through Bermuda to Brazil, and in the eastern Atlantic at Ascension Island, St. Helena, and surrounding areas.

Size: Captive adults seldom exceed 36 to 40 inches, though tales of 48 to 50 inch monsters in the wild are not uncommon.

Natural Habitat: Able to thrive in a variety of habitats, the Spotted Moray is one of the most versatile and adaptable species known. While fond of rocky shallows and sheltered reefs, the Spotted Moray's favorite haunts are grassy seabeds and leeward sandbars. Although common in waist-deep tidal flats, this species also thrives at depths ranging down to an impressive 220 meters!

Diet & Feeding: Active and taking prey at all points of the clock, a hungry Spotted Moray will slip out of hiding and swim freely—not hugging the reef or seafloor like other eels—into open water in search of prey. These eels have even been seen hunting in conjunction with other predators such as Coneys and other sea basses. Although it is yet unexplained, a strange behavior is worth noting here. As it sits in its hideaway with only its head exposed, the Spotted Moray attracts sea bass, which will rest on the coral beside the eel's head and rapidly flick their caudal fins back and forth. Even more astounding is the fact that when one bass tires from its flitting motions and swims away, another is already on line to resume the bizarre dance. There is some speculation that this dance is an invitation for the eel to go on the hunt, for when it does so, the frightened, scattering fish fleeing from the eel grow careless and make easy pickings for the bass.

Description: A moderately sized species, the Spotted Moray has a base color of golden to yellow or even ivory-white, and is heavily accented with overlapping spots, blotches, and speckles of gray-black to brown or purple. The high dorsal fin adds to the lateral compression, and makes this species a very powerful swimmer. The Spotted Moray has large, pronounced eyes and, because it is a diurnal hunter, most likely has eyesight far superior to other morays.

Aquarium Suitability: 1.

Special Conditions: Best kept by *highly advanced marine experts*. Because of this eel's wide-roaming foraging habits, it needs excessively large quarters, over 400 gallons, at least.

Gymnothorax pictus / **Peppered Moray**

Minimum Tank Size: 180 gallons.

Range: Throughout southern Pacific and Indo-Pacific regions: Red Sea and coastal Africa east through Galapagos and Coco Islands, north through Ryukyu and Hawaii, south through Micronesia and Australian waters.

Size: Up to 56 inches TL.

Natural Habitat: Reef-associated dwellings. Found amid rocky outcroppings, rubble-strewn sand flats, ship wreckages, and open-water atolls.

Diet & Feeding: One of the most aggressive of all the morays when it comes to feeding, this species is known to actually leave the water to procure food. Fish and shrimps in landlocked tidal pools often fall victim to the Peppered Moray's appetites, as do crabs crawling along seaside rocks! Favored food items include all small fish and crustaceans. An active predator and powerful swimmer, this eel has been recorded as chasing schools of fish in open water. Feeds both day and night.

Description: A thick-bodied species with high dorsal fin and laterally compressed body for speed in the water, the Peppered Moray sports a base color of dark gray to black, and is speckled in irregular darker blotches. Blotches typically smaller and more tightly arranged on the head and jaws. This unique dark-on-dark blotching makes for a rippled effect, the moray's skin looking just like flowing water. Jaw muscles pronounced at rear of head, and the slender jaws are arched for snagging swimming fish. Nares are pronounced, but only slightly.

Aquarium Suitability: 4.

Special Conditions: Because this species is prone to leaping to catch prey in the wild, it will certainly not abandon such behaviors in your tank. Take especial care when feeding, for an overanxious Peppered Moray may well leap clean out of your tank when you approach at feeding time. Secure your tank against possible escapes and leaps by keeping the ornaments and short live rock low in the tank. Tall standing live rock may give the impression of a coastline, which the eel will recognize as a source of food. Such high structures may actually encourage the animal's jumping behavior.

Gymnothorax prasinus / **Yellow Moray**

Minimum Tank Size: 125 gallons

Range: Native to the Southwest Pacific immediately surrounding New Zealand and southern Australia.

Size: Though most individuals do not exceed 36 inches, the occasional Yellow Moray may reach 40 inches long.

Natural Habitat: A true recluse, this eel spends more time tucked away in the safety of the reef than most others, emerging only at night to forage. Haunts include holes, crevasses, caves, and overhangs within the reef and adjoining substrata. Also favors grassy beds and seaweed entanglements. This eel frequents both shallow and deeper offshore environments.

Diet & Feeding: Crabs, crabs, and more crabs. The wild diet of the Yellow Moray is primarily comprised of different species of crabs, though sleeping or careless fish are taken on occasion. When it forages at night, the Yellow Moray rarely strays far from the reef. Rather, it noses in and out of tight holes and caverns within the reef in search of errant crustaceans. Often patrols stands of seaweed, where it is supremely camouflaged from both predator and prey.

Description: Often referred to as the Green Moray, this species is not to be confused with *G. funebris* of the Atlantic Ocean. The head is surprisingly blunt to be a member of the *Gymnothorax* genus, though the dentition is quite formidable. Elongate nares protrude from sunken nasal pits, and the eyes are somewhat reduced in this strictly nocturnal hunter. A shy and retiring animal, the Yellow Moray has been, in my experience, quicker to retreat from the hand of an intruder than to attack. However, if sorely molested or cornered, it will not hesitate to lash out violently against its attacker.

Aquarium Suitability: 4.

Special Conditions: Use caution when mixing this species with a reef tank, as the Yellow Moray produced a copious amount of nitrogenous waste and may pollute the tank beyond what the coral polyps can tolerate.

Gymnothorax undulatus / **Undulated Moray**

Minimum Tank Size: 200 gallons.

Range: Widespread throughout Indian and Pacific Oceans, Red Sea and eastern Africa, east to French Polynesia and Micronesia, north through the Sea of Japan, south through Great Barrier Reef, and eastward as far as the coasts of Panama and Costa Rica.

Size: Up to 60 inches.

Natural Habitat: Common along reef shoals and other rubble-strewn areas such as lagoons and bays. Also favors seaward caves, overhangs, and rocky trenches.

Diet & Feeding: A nocturnal hunter, the Undulated Moray preys almost exclusively on sleeping fish and octopuses. This eel ventures deep into underwater caverns, spending perhaps 90 percent of its time there, foraging for food. Using its slender snout and needle-like teeth, the Undulated Moray noses in and out of crevasses, rooting out and devouring whatever it finds.

Description: Base color is a rich green to black crisscrossed in undulating lines of yellow to golden or even white in some specimens. Snout and lower jaw often lighter than the rest of the body. The long teeth and curved jaws are highly adapted to feeding on fish. High dorsal fin and laterally compressed body add power and speed when swimming, suggesting this animal is an adept hunter, actively pursuing its prey. Reports of ciguatera poisoning are common for this species.

Aquarium Suitability: 3.

Special Conditions: If you do keep an Undulated Moray, be sure to anchor all rockwork within the tank, as this powerful eel can undermine and topple most structures. Good tank mates include adult Volitans Lionfish *(Pterois volitans)*, as the poisonous fins of this species will help keep them safe from the ravenous jaws of the Undulated Moray, while a grouper of the same size might well become dinner.

Muraena helena / **Mediterranean Moray**

Minimum Tank Size: 150 gallons.

Range: Eastern Atlantic and Mediterranean Sea. British Isles south to Senegal, Cape Verde, the Canary Islands, and surrounding areas.

Size: Up to 60 inches.

Natural Habitat: Strongly reef associated, the Mediterranean Moray frequents inshore lagoons and the fringes of sheltered reefs and open water. Lives most of its life in shallow waters, rarely venturing deeper than 50 meters. Throughout the Mediterranean Sea, this moray is quite common, and is frequently encountered by divers investigating old Greek pots and urns lost in shipwrecks.

Diet & Feeding: Lying quietly coiled under a rock or in a crevasse, the Mediterranean Moray has the curious habit of striking its prey, grasping it in its vise-like jaws, then recoiling, drawing its victim back into its lair. Favored food items include small fish and crustaceans, while squid are at the top of the menu. Octopuses are also taken. Nocturnal.

Description: Head and jaws are brownish to charcoal gray or even purplish. Body is a base gray to purplish, with numerous yellow blotches aligned in loosely longitudinal rows. Smaller blotches may fuse to form a snowflake-like pattern. High dorsal fin with laterally compressed body. The jaws are slightly arched to accommodate feeding. Teeth are moderately long and sharp. Anterior nares pronounced, posterior nares (directly above the eyes) are present, but less pronounced. A dark band crosses the head between the eye sockets.

Aquarium Suitability: 5.

Special Conditions: This species thrives in tanks with plenty of open-water and sandy substrata. Tight, enclosed environments, such as elaborate reef tanks, are very unlike the Mediterranean's natural habitat, and may cause undue stress if the eel does not have room to swim, and stretch-out. A good setup for a Mediterranean Moray would have most of the structure/coral/live rock toward one end of the tank, leaving the other half open to swim freely.

Muraena lentiginosa / **Jewel Moray**

Minimum Tank Size: 75 gallons.

Range: Eastern Pacific from Baja, California south through coastal Peru, and seaward to the Galapagos Islands.

Size: A diminutive species, the Jewel Moray seldom exceeds 23 inches in the wild. Captive specimens may thrive for years before attaining lengths of even 15 to 18 inches.

Natural Habitat: Powerfully nocturnal, these morays spend their days tucked in tight fissures within the reef. Other diurnal retreats include reef overhangs, snags, rock-strewn flats, seaward cliffs, caves, and intertidal flats.

Diet & Feeding: After sunset, the Jewel Moray leaves the shelter of the reef and goes on the hunt for any and every moving creature it can subdue. On the menu are crabs, shrimps, recently molted lobsters, squids, octopuses, and any fish that is small enough or defenseless enough to be swallowed.

Description: A laterally compressed animal, the Jewel Moray sports a very large head, which may comprise as much as 15 percent of total body length. The jaws are very narrow and moderately hooked, indicating this eel has a knack for rooting fish and large shrimps out of crevasses within the reef. The laterally flattened teeth are backwardly curved and are exceedingly sharp, as are the conical vomerine teeth. One of the more attractive morays, the Jewel wears a basecoat of light to chocolate brown or even purplish. Body and head are speckled in round spots or ocelli of golden to pale yellow. Anterior and posterior nares somewhat pronounced.

Aquarium Suitability: 5.

Special Conditions: A copious amount of rockwork and hideaways are necessary when housing a Jewel Moray. This species is easily stressed by boisterous or very large tankmates, and will likely refuse food to the point of starvation if it is uncomfortable or insecure in its environs. Living corals and macro-algae make for very secure surroundings.

Rhinomuraena quaesita / **Ribbon Moray**

Minimum Tank Size: 100 gallons.

Range: All throughout the Indo-Pacific: eastern coast of Africa, east through Micronesia, north through the Sea of Japan, and south to New Caledonia. Very common throughout much of this range, especially in Indonesian waters.

Size: May exceed 50 to 53 inches, though such specimens are rare. Captive lengths seldom exceed 40 to 45 inches.

Natural Habitat: Devout, yet highly secretive reef dweller. The Ribbon Moray thrives in warm, clear waters, and almost never ventures deeper than 50 meters down.

Diet & Feeding: Dines on very small fishes, and minuscule crustaceans. Recently molted shrimps and small crabs are taken with much gusto in the wild, though these eels tend to shy away from such items in captivity.

Description: Perhaps the most curious of all morays, the Ribbon Moray's body is midnight black as a juvenile, while the fused dorsal/caudal fin is whitish to pale yellow. This striking contrast makes the Ribbon Moray one of the most aesthetically stunning eels on the market today. As the animal matures, its black color will lighten into a rich, cobalt blue, while the whiteness of its fins will deepen into a golden yellow. With further maturation, the blue males will change sex and appearance to become bright yellow females! Head is elongate with greatly exaggerated nares, which flare out like an open flower or the bell of a trumpet. Fleshy, whisker-like protuberances extend from the chin. The eyes are small, but this eel's heightened sense of smell makes it a formidable predator. Teeth are small, but sharp for piercing the scales of its fishy prey.

Aquarium Suitability: 1.

Special Conditions: Easily the daintiest of all the morays, captive Ribbon Morays feed almost exclusively on freshwater mollies (*Poecilia* spp.) in captivity, and may refuse other fare altogether. Fortunately, mollies purchased in bulk are relatively inexpensive, and can easily be acclimated to the saltwater environment over a period of two to three days. So leaving a school of mollies in your tank and allowing the skittish Ribbon Moray to feed at its own leisure is your best bet. When the molly population dwindles every few weeks, simply restock the tank.

Scuticaria tigrina / **Tiger Reef Moray**

Minimum Tank Size: 100 gallons.

Range: Extremely widespread across the Indian and Pacific Oceans: eastern coast of Africa east through Indo-Pacific and Micronesia, and eastward still to western Mexico, south through Costa Rica and Panama.

Size: Up to 48 inches long.

Natural Habitat: As its name suggests, this species favors sandy seabeds, sheltered lagoons, seaward reefs, and other rock-strewn areas.

Diet & Feeding: The Tiger Reef Moray employs a feeding strategy of stealth and lightening speed. By hugging the bottom and snaking its way between the rocks and coral outcroppings of its native environment, the Tiger Reef Moray stalks up on feeding crabs and unsuspecting fishes. This eel is inordinately patient in the hunt, and may lay, unmoving, just inches from its prey, waiting for just the right moment to strike. Frequently taken prey includes crabs, shrimps, and bottom-dwelling fish species.

Description: Certainly an anomaly among the morays, the Tiger Reef Moray is odd looking on all counts. The head is short and the snout is rounded. Eyes and dorsal/caudal fins are greatly reduced. Mouth is quite small, and the dentition is not as sharp as that of the *Gymnothorax* species. The jaws are strong and can easily crush struggling prey or inflict a painful bite to a human hand. Highly camouflaged amid the rocks and sand of the sea floor, the Tiger Reef Moray is yellow to burnt-umber brown with numerous spots and blotches of various sizes. Spots are black to purple and are rimmed in yellow. Speckles dominate head, while larger blotches cover the body.

Aquarium Suitability: 4.

Special Conditions: The Tiger Reef Moray needs a very specialized habitat in the aquarium. Thick substrate of sand mixed with crushed coral, and numerous isolated rocky outcroppings situated throughout the tank will closely simulate the eel's preferred natural environment. This eel is extremely secretive, and will only emerge during the darkest hours of the night. It requires very dim lighting and deep retreats in which it can escape into near total darkness during the daytime.

Siderea griseus / **Gray Moray**

Minimum Tank Size: 125 gallons.

Range: Found throughout the Red Sea and in the shallows of the western Indian Ocean.

Size: One of the smaller of the *Gymnothorax* species (the genus *Siderea* is considered by many to be an unsubstantiated off-shoot of *Gymnothorax*), the Gray Moray grows to a wild maximum of just under three feet long, and may stay considerably smaller in captivity, adults seldom exceeding 24 inches.

Natural Habitat: A staunch reef-dweller, the Gray Moray favors heavily sheltered areas: coral caves, reef overhangs, ship wreckage, leeward sea cliffs, lagoons, sounds, bays, and boulder-strewn shallows.

Diet & Feeding: Because of its reef-centric lifestyle, the Gray Moray is adept at preying upon the many-legged things in the ocean. Its favorite prey includes crabs, shrimps, lobsters, and all manner of cephalopods. Small fish are also taken on occasion.

Description: Sporting a beautiful base color of pale whitish to charcoal gray or even pinkish, this eel's head is adorned with darker lines and dashes arranged in seemingly geometric triangles and diamonds, thereby earning this eels the alternate name "Geometric Moray." The head is typically a darker shade than the rest of the body, with the eyes being a striking silver tone or pure white. The back of the head is equipped with powerful jaw muscles, and is noticeably denoted from the neck. It has a very high dorsal fin. Nares moderately pronounced. Has short vomerine teeth as well as rows of teeth in the upper and lower jaws for subduing struggling prey.

Aquarium Suitability: A definite 5.

Special Conditions: Although it is reef safe around sessile invertebrates, the Gray Moray is a crustacean's worst nightmare. Virtually all motile invertebrates and any fishes less than 7 inches TL are potential meals for an adult Gray Moray. These are best housed with large fish species or in crustacean-free reef tanks.

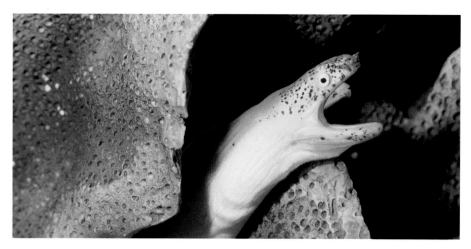

Uropterygius concolor / **Unicolor Snake Moray**

Minimum Tank Size: 55 gallons.

Range: Throughout the Indo-Pacific region. Red Sea and coastal Africa east to southern Japan, south to New Caledonia and Micronesia.

Size: One of the smallest of all the morays, the Unicolor Snake Moray grows to a diminutive 20 inches.

Natural Habitat: A highly adaptable species, the Unicolor Snake Moray is found in a wide range of habitats, ranging from shallow, offshore reefs to brackish lagoons, river estuaries, and mangrove swamps.

Diet & Feeding: Wild diet consists primarily of small invertebrates: minute crabs, shrimps, fingerling cephalopods, and especially small fishes. Within the microenvironment of the mangrove, however, this eel is a top predator. Mangroves, with their shallow waters and dense networks of stone and vegetation, act as nurseries for the developing young of large fish species.

Description: Drab olive to light yellowish or tan-brown base accented with pale spots and a dorsal/caudal fin that is often trimmed in light yellow to off-white. Juveniles are more brightly colored than adults. Eyes are large and well developed, indicating this eel is a visual hunter, relying more heavily on its sight than most other morays. Mouth is relatively small, with slightly pronounced nares. Teeth sharp and angled slightly backwards to aid in piercing and hanging onto prey.

Aquarium Suitability: 3.

Special Conditions: Because this moray comes from a variety of habitats, it can be very difficult to match your home aquarium with the exact native habitat from which an imported specimen came. For example, you have a 75-gallon reef tank and your local pet shop receives a shipment of Unicolor Snake Morays from a brackish river delta near southern Asia. If you purchase one of these eels, it will not likely live long in your tank, as it may never have seen a coral reef in its life, and is certainly not accustomed to such an alien environment. If possible, set up an aquarium that mimics perfectly the eel's *specific* habitat. Make sure your importer sends you an eel that will thrive in your home aquarium, which may have to be a mangrove or brackish tank in order to accommodate a Unicolor Snake Moray. In a nutshell, a successful Unicolor Snake Moray endeavor involves far more planning and knowledge than that of any other moray species.

Catalogue to Additional Species of Moray Eels

While the previous pages exhibit many of the more-popular moray species, the following will briefly introduce you to some of the less-commonly available ones. As our wonderful hobby advances and remote seas and oceans become more accessible, we will certainly find more species and morphs making their way into the aquariums of marine hobbyists.

Should you be fortunate enough to have one of these species already, you can probably assume that the care requirements are the same as for the most closely-related species to your own. It may be difficult to get this information, however with the vast resources that are available to hobbyists today you'll find your search to ultimately be rewarding and educational at the same time. This book contains a resources section and that is a good place to start. Of course, there are many more places to find fascinating moray information than just what's contained herein. Let this book be just the foundation for which the rest of your moray knowledge is built upon.

Gymnothorax **sp.**

Gymnothorax **sp.**

Gymnothorax prionodon

Enchelycore **sp. aff.** *bayeri*

Popular Species

Gymnothorax tile

Gymnothorax miliaris

Gymnothorax nudivomer

Gymnothorax permistus

Gymnothorax zonipectus

Gymnothorax castaneus

Keeping Moray Eels in Aquariums

Gymnothorax mordax

Gymnothorax ramosus

Gymnothorax woodwardi

Gymnothorax javanicus

Gymnothorax rueppelliae

Gymnothorax breedeni

Appendix I

The following is a complete list of all known moray eel species. At least, it was complete at the time I wrote, as Latin nomenclature and speciation has a tendency to change overnight. Several "old school" moray species may appear to be omitted, and some species-purists may get their hackles raised at the very notion that this list is "complete," but as time has passed, many different species have been re-described and re-classified as sub-species, or as isolated populations of a larger species. So listed here are the current genus and species names, dates these animals were first described, and by whom. Note that the common names included here may vary from one location to the next. For example, the Snowflake Moray is known as the "Starry" or "Diamondback" Moray in certain circles, but the Latin, *Echidna nebulosa*, is universal. Likewise, many species, which I have labeled "No Common Name," in fact may have any number of little-known common names given them by local fishermen or indigenous peoples.

Anarchias allardicei (Jordan & Starks, 1906)	Allardice's Moray
Anarchias cantonensis (Schultz, 1943)	Canton Isle Moray
Anarchias euryurus (Vaillant, 1919)	No Common Name
Anarchias galapagensis (Seale, 1940)	Minute Moray
Anarchias leucurus (Snyder, 1904)	Snyder's Moray
Anarchias longicaudis (Peters, 1877)	No Common Name
Anarchias maldiviensis (Klausewitz, 1964)	No Common Name
Anarchias seychellensis (Smith, 1962)	Seychelles Moray
Anarchias similis (Lea, 1913)	Pygmy Moray
Channomuraena vittata (Saldanha & Quèro, 1994)	Broad-Banded Moray
Cirrimaxilla formosa (Chen & Shao, 1995)	No Common Name
Echidna amblyodon (Bleeker, 1856)	No Common Name
Echidna catenata (Bleeker, 1856)	Chain Moray
Echidna delicatula (Kaup, 1856)	Mottled Moray
Echidna leucotaenia (Schultz, 1943)	Ivory-Faced Moray

Echidna nebulosa (Bleeker, 1853)	Snowflake Moray
Echidna nocturna (Cope, 1872)	Freckled Moray
Echidna peli (Kaup, 1856)	Pebble-Tooth Moray
Echidna polyzona (Jenkins, 1903)	Barred Moray
Echidna rhodochilus (Bleeker, 1863)	No Common Name
Echidna unicolor (Schultz, 1953)	Brown Moray
Echidna xanthospilos (Bleeker, 1859)	No Common Name
Enchelycore anatina (Lowe, 1838)	Fang-Tooth Moray
Enchelycore bayeri (Schultz, 1953)	Hook-Jaw Moray
Enchelycore bikiniensis (Schultz, 1953)	Bikini Atoll Moray
Enchelycore carychroa (Böhlke & Böhlke, 1976)	Chestnut Moray
Enchelycore kamara (Böhlke & Böhlke, 1980)	Dark-Spotted Moray
Enchelycore lichenosa (Snyder, 1901)	Reticulate Hook-Jaw Moray
Enchelycore nigricans (Gronow, 1854)	Mulatto Conger
Enchelycore nycturnaus (Smith, 2002)	No Common Name
Enchelycore octivania (Myers & Wade, 1941)	Slender Jaw Moray
Enchelycore pardalis (Jordan & Evermann, 1903)	Dragon Moray
Enchelycore ramosa (Griffin, 1926)	Mosaic Moray
Enchelycore schismatorhynchus (Bleeker, 1853)	White-Margin Moray
Enchelynassa canina (Quoy & Gaimard, 1824)	Viper Moray
Gymnomuraena zebra (Kaup, 1856)	Zebra Moray
Gymnothorax afer (Bloch, 1795 & Günther, 1870)	Dark Moray
Gymnothorax albimarginatus (Schlegel, 1846)	White-Margin Moray
Gymnothorax angusticauda (Weber & de Beaufort, 1916)	No Common Name
Gymnothorax angusticeps (Hildebrand & Barton, 1949)	No Common Name
Gymnothorax annasona (Whitley, 1937)	No Common Name
Gymnothorax annulatus (Smith & Böhlke, 1997)	Banded Moray
Gymnothorax atolli (Pietschmann, 1935)	Atoll Moray
Gymnothorax australicola (Lavenberg, 1992)	No Common Name
Gymnothorax austrinus (Böhlke & McCosker, 2001)	Southern Moray

Gymnothorax bacalladoi (Böhlke & Brito, 1987)	No Common Name
Gymnothorax bathyphilus (Randall & McCosker, 1975)	No Common Name
Gymnothorax berndti (Snyder, 1904)	Y-Patterned Moray
Gymnothorax breedeni (McCosker & Randall, 1977)	Black-Cheek Moray
Gymnothorax buroensis (Bleeker, 1857)	Vagrant Moray
Gymnothorax castaneus (Jordan & Gilbert, 1883)	No Common Name
Gymnothorax castlei (Böhlke & Randall, 1999)	No Common Name
Gymnothorax cephalospilus (Böhlke & McCosker, 2001)	Head-Spot Moray
Gymnothorax chilospilus (Bleeker, 1865)	Lip-Spot Moray
Gymnothorax chlamydatus (Snyder, 1908)	No Common Name
Gymnothorax conspersus (Poey, 1867)	Saddled Moray
Gymnothorax cribrorsis (Whitley, 1932)	Sieve-Patterned Moray
Gymnothorax dorsalis (Seale, 1917)	No Common Name
Gymnothorax dovii (Günther, 1870)	Speckled Moray
Gymnothorax elegans (Bliss, 1883)	Elegant Moray
Gymnothorax enigmaticus (McCosker & Randall, 1982)	Enigma Moray
Gymnothorax equatorialis (Hildebrand, 1946)	Spotted-Tail Moray
Gymnothorax eurostus (Abbott, 1861)	Abbott's Moray
Gymnothorax eurygnathus (Böhlke, 2001)	No Common Name
Gymnothorax favagineus (Bloch & Schneider, 1801)	Laced Moray
Gymnothorax fimbriatus (Richardson, 1848)	Fimbricated Moray
Gymnothorax flavimarginatus (Rüppell, 1830)	Yellow-Edged Moray
Gymnothorax flavoculus (Böhlke & Randall, 1996)	Palenose Moray
Gymnothorax formosus (Bleeker, 1865)	No Common Name
Gymnothorax funebris (Ranzani, 1840)	Green Moray
Gymnothorax fuscomaculatus (Schultz, 1953)	Brown-Spotted Moray
Gymnothorax gracilicauda (Jenkins, 1903)	Slender-Tail Moray
Gymnothorax griseus (Lacepède, 1803)	Geometric Moray
Gymnothorax hepaticus (Rüppell, 1830)	No Common Name

Gymnothorax hepaticus (Rüppell, 1830) — Liver-Colored Moray

Gymnothorax herri (Herre, 1923) — No Common Name

Gymnothorax hubbsi (Böhlke & Böhlke, 1977) — Lichen Moray

Gymnothorax insingteena (Richardson, 1845) — No Common Name

Gymnothorax intesi (Fourmanoir & Rivaton, 1979) — No Common Name

Gymnothorax javanicus (Bleeker, 1859) — Giant Moray

Gymnothorax johnsoni (Bliss, 1883) — White-Spotted Moray

Gymnothorax kikado (Temminck & Schlegel, 1846) — Kikado Moray

Gymnothorax kolpos (Böhlke & Böhlke, 1980) — Blacktail Moray

Gymnothorax kontodontos (Böhlke, 2000) — No Common Name

Gymnothorax longiquus (Whitley, 1848) — No Common Name

Gymnothorax maderensis (Johnson, 1862) — Sharktooth Moray

Gymnothorax mareei (Poll, 1953) — Spot-Jaw Moray

Gymnothorax margaritophorus (Bleeker, 1865) — Blotchneck Moray

Gymnothorax marshallensis (Schultz, 1953) — Marshall Island Moray

Gymnothorax mccockeri (Smith & Böhlke, 1997) — No Common Name

Gymnothorax megaspilus (Böhlke & Randall, 1995) — Oman Moray

Gymnothorax melatremus (Schultz, 1953) — Dwarf Moray

Gymnothorax meleagris (Kaup, 1856) — Turkey Moray

Gymnothorax micorspila (Günther, 1870) — No Common Name

Gymnothorax microstictus (Böhlke, 2000) — No Common Name

Gymnothorax miliaris (Mowbray, 1931) — Golden Tail Moray

Gymnothorax minor (Temminck & Schlegel, 1846) — No Common Name

Gymnothorax moluccensis (Bleeker, 1865) — Moluccan Moray

Gymnothorax monochrous (Bleeker, 1865) — Drab Moray

Gymnothorax monostigma (Regan, 1909) — One-Spot Moray

Gymnothorax mordax (Ayers, 1859) — California Moray

Gymnothorax moringa (Evermann & Marsh, 1900) — Spotted Moray

Gymnothorax mucifer (Snyder, 1904) — No Common Name

Gymnothorax nasuta (de Buen, 1961) — No Common Name

Gymnothorax neglectus (Tanaka, 1911) — No Common Name

Gymnothorax nigromarginatus (Girard, 1858) — Black-Edged Moray

Gymnothorax niphostigmus (Chen & Shao, 1996)	Snowflake-Patched Moray
Gymnothorax nubilus (Richardson, 1848)	Grey Moray
Gymnothorax nudivomer (Seale, 1917)	Starry Moray
Gymnothorax nuttingi (Snyder, 1904)	No Common Name
Gymnothorax obesus (Whitley & Phillipps, 1939)	Griffin's Moray
Gymnothorax ocellatus (Evermann & Marsh, 1899)	Caribbean Moray
Gymnothorax panamensis (Steindachner, 1876)	Panamic Moray
Gymnothorax parini (Smith & Böhlke, 1991)	No Common Name
Gymnothorax phalarus (Bussing, 1998)	No Common Name
Gymnothorax phasmatodes (Smith, 1962)	Phantom Moray
Gymnothorax philippinus (Jordan & Seale, 1907)	No Common Name
Gymnothorax pictus (Ahl, 1789)	Peppered Moray
Gymnothorax pikei (Bliss, 1883)	Pike's Moray
Gymnothorax pindae (Smith, 1962)	Pinda Moray
Gymnothorax polygonus (Poey, 1875)	Polygon Moray
Gymnothorax polyspondylus (Böhlke & Randall, 2000)	No Common Name
Gymnothorax polyuranodon (Bleeker, 1853)	Freshwater Moray
Gymnothorax porphyreus (Günther, 1872)	No Common Name
Gymnothorax prasinus (Günther, 1870)	Yellow Moray
Gymnothorax prionodon (Jordan & Richardson, 1909)	Mottled Australian Moray
Gymnothorax prismodon (Böhlke & Randall, 2000)	No Common Name
Gymnothorax prolatus (Sasaki & Amaoka, 1991)	No Common Name
Gymnothorax pseudoherri (Böhlke, 2000)	No Common Name
Gymnothorax pseudothyrsoideus (Bleeker, 1852)	Highfin Moray
Gymnothorax punctatofasciatus (Bleeker, 1863)	No Common Name
Gymnothorax punctatus (Bloch & Schneider, 1801)	Red Sea Spotted Moray
Gymnothorax randalli (Smith & Böhlke, 1997)	No Common Name
Gymnothorax reevesii (Richardson, 1845)	No Common Name
Gymnothorax reticularis (Bloch, 1795)	No Common Name
Gymnothorax richardsonii (Bleeker, 1852)	Richardson's Moray
Gymnothorax robinsi (Böhlke, 1997)	No Common Name

Gymnothorax rueppellii (Bleeker, 1856)	Banded Moray
Gymnothorax sagenodeta (Richardson, 1848)	No Common Name
Gymnothorax sagmacephalus (Böhlke, 1997)	No Common Name
Gymnothorax saxicola (Jordan & Davis, 1891)	Ocellated Moray
Gymnothorax serratidens (Hildebrand & Barton, 1949)	No Common Name
Gymnothorax sokotrensis (Kotthaus, 1968)	No Common Name
Gymnothorax steindachneri (Jordan & Evermann, 1903)	Steindachner's Moray
Gymnothorax thyrsoideus (Bleeker, 1853)	Grey-Faced Moray
Gymnothorax tile (Hamilton, 1822)	No Common Name
Gymnothorax undulatus (Richardson, 1848)	Undulated Moray
Gymnothorax unicolor (Risso, 1810)	Brown Moray
Gymnothorax vagrans (Seale, 1917)	No Common Name
Gymnothorax verrilli (Jordan & Gilbert, 1883)	White-Edged Moray
Gymnothorax vicinus (Kaup, 1860)	Purplemouth Moray
Gymnothorax vicinus (Stromann, 1896)	Green Moray
Gymnothorax woodwardi (McCulloch, 1912)	No Common Name
Gymnothorax ypsilon (Hatooka & Randall, 1992)	Y-Bar Moray
Gymnothorax zonipectis (Seale, 1906)	Barred-Fin Moray
Monopenchelys acuta (Parr, 1930)	Red-Faced Moray
Muraena appendiculata (Guichenot, 1848)	No Common Name
Muraena argus (Steindachner, 1870)	Argus Moray
Muraena australiae (Richardson, 1848)	No Common Name
Muraena clepsydra (Gilbert, 1898)	Hourglass Moray
Muraena helena (Johnson, 1862)	Mediterranean Moray
Muraena insularum (Jordan & Davis, 1891)	No Common Name
Muraena lentiginosa (Jenyns, 1842)	Jewel Moray
Muraena melanotis (Pfaff, 1933)	Honeycomb Moray
Muraena pavonina (Richardson, 1845)	Whitespot Moray
Muraena retifera (Goode & Bean, 1882)	Reticulate Moray
Muraena robusta (Rubinoff, 1966)	Robust Moray

Pseudoechidna brummeri (Bleeker, 1859)	White-Ribbon Moray
Rhinomuraena quaesita (Barbour, 1908)	Ribbon Moray
Scuticaria okinawae (Regan, 1903)	Short-Tailed Snake Moray
Scuticaria tigrina (Lesson, 1828)	Tiger Reef Moray
Strophidon sathete (Bleeker, 1854)	Slender Giant Moray
Uropterygius concolor (Rüppell, 1838)	Unicolor Snake Moray
Uropterygius fascicolatus (Regan, 1909)	Blotched Moray
Uropterygius fuscoguttatus (Schultz, 1953)	Brown-Spotted Snake Moray
Uropterygius genie (McCosker & Smith, 1997)	No Common Name
Uropterygius golanii (Randall & Golani, 1995)	No Common Name
Uropterygius inornatus (Gosline, 1958)	Drab Snake Moray
Uropterygius kamar (McCosker & Randall, 1977)	Bar-Lip Reef Moray
Uropterygius macrocephalus (Jordan & Starck, 1906)	Needle-Tooth Moray
Uropterygius macularis (Böhlke, 1967)	Marbled Moray
Uropterygius makatei (Gosline, 1958)	No Common Name
Uropterygius marmoratus (Lacepède, 1803)	Marble Reef Moray
Uropterygius micropterus (Bleeker, 1852)	Tidal Pool Snake Moray
Uropterygius nagoensis (Hatooka, 1984)	No Common Name
Uropterygius polyspilus (Regan, 1909)	Large-Spotted Snake Moray
Uropterygius polystictus (Myers & Wade, 1941)	Many-Spotted Snake Moray
Uropterygius supraforatus (Regan, 1909)	Many-Toothed Snake Moray
Uropterygius versutus (Bussing, 1991)	Two-Holes Moray
Uropterygius wheeleri (Blache, 1967)	No Common Name
Uropterygius xanthopterus (Smith, 1962)	Freckled-Faced Moray
Uropterygius xenodontus (McCosker & Smith, 1997)	Black Snake Moray

Appendix II

As is true with most pet types, there are certain species that should not be considered for captivity. Birds make fine pets, but housing a Turkey Vulture may not be the best idea. Likewise, there are millions of dog owners worldwide, yet allowing your personal pack of Hyenas to run amok in the neighborhood is just not advisable. The same holds true for the morays. Some make great pets, while others are less-than-desirable. The following species should be avoided by hobbyists at the beginning to moderate skill level, and should be approached with a healthy amount of caution by advanced hobbyists and professionals. Species labeled "Traumatogenic" tend to be ill-tempered and are more than capable of inflicting deep, serious wounds that are excruciatingly painful, prone to infection, and which take a long time healing. Species labeled "Ciguatera Poison" have, due to their diet in the wild, accumulated dangerous levels of common reef toxins in their blood, flesh, and saliva. Ciguatera poisoning is sometimes known as "reef-poisoning," and usually come from eating contaminated flesh. A bite from a ciguatera-prone species is *reputed* to be enough to contract the poison. Symptoms include nausea, fever, localized swelling, giddiness, comatose, and in rare cases, death.

Echidna rhodochilus	No Common Name	Traumatogenic
Enchelycore bayeri	Hookjaw Moray	Traumatogenic
E. canina	Viper Moray	Traumatogenic
Gymnothorax breedeni	Black-cheek Moray	Traumatogenic
G. favagineus	Blackspotted Moray	Ciguatera Poison
G. flavimarginatus	Yellow-edged Moray	Ciguatera Poison
G. funebris	Green Moray	Traumatogenic

G. javanicus	Giant Moray	Ciguatera Poison
G. kidako	No Common Name	Traumatogenic
G. meleagris	Turkey Moray	Ciguatera Poison
G. mordax	California Moray	Traumatogenic
G. moringa	Spotted Moray	Traumatogenic
G. nudivomer	Starry Moray	Exudes Toxic Mucus
G. pictus	Peppered Moray	Ciguatera Poison
G. polyurandon	Freshwater Moray	Ciguatera Poison
G. reticularis	No Common Name	Traumatogenic
G. rueppelliae	Banded Moray	Unknown
G. undulatus	Undulated Moray	Ciguatera Poison
G. vicinus	Purple-mouth Moray	Traumatogenic
Muraena helena	Mediterranean Moray	Traumatogenic
Strophidon sathete	Slender Giant Moray	Traumatogenic

Appendix III

If the entire contents of this book had to be summarized in one page, this would be it. The following is what I call the "Universal Moray Eel Care Sheet." If you are confused on an issue, follow these conditions until you can find the answers you seek. Ideal quarantine tanks will also operate under these conditions.

Temperature:	73 to 78 degrees Fahrenheit
pH:	8.2 to 8.3
Water Changes:	No less then 15% every week. Siphon substrate.
Salinity:	1.022-1.025
Diet:	Offer shrimp, squid, silversides, mollies, clam, mussel, mysis, krill, cut fish, or crab meat twice a week.
Ammonia:	Zero.
Nitrites:	Zero.
Nitrates:	Zero.
Phosphorous:	10ppm or less.
Lighting:	Subdued, only enough to accommodate viewing.
Filtration:	Cycle at least 8x volume per hour using canister filters and powerheads. Activated carbon and efficient protein skimming are essential.
In-Tank Current:	Moderate to strong, angle powerheads into center of tank.
Tank Security:	High. Leave no gaps or openings in lid.

Quarantine tanks must not have activated carbon if the water column contains medication.

Appendix IV

The following is a list of diseases and their respective symptoms and treatments. Diagnosis of malady in a moray eel is never an easy thing, and I highly recommend the reading of the **Diseases & Disorders** chapter in this book before making a diagnosis of your moray. Serious water changes and improvements in husbandry practices are recommended with every malady.

Symptoms	Disorder	Treatment
Tiny white spots covering body; resembles dusting of salt. Rubbing against substrate or décor.	White Spot Disease, Saltwater ICK.	Quarantine, conduct a 10-12 minute freshwater dip, treat with 37% Formalin at a dosage of 1 drop per gallon.
Tiny worms, specks, leeches, dots, or other things clinging to the skin, head, or gills. Rubbing against tank décor.	External Parasites.	Quarantine. Conduct a 10-12 minute freshwater dip. Treat with 37% Formalin at a dosage of 1 drop per gallon. Perform a 15% water change daily until symptoms disappear.
Loss of appetite, increased appetite with no growth, exaggerated breathing, irregular bowl movements, loss of color, listlessness, visible parasites extruding from anus.	Internal Parasites.	Quarantine. Treat with Flabendazole, Piperazine, Flagyl, or Metronidazole. Increase aeration and feedings. Medicated food may be necessary. Perform a 15% water change daily.

Bruises, lesions, cuts, scrapes, nicks, etc.	External Wounds	Quarantine if serious and watch closely for secondary infections—especially fungus infections.
Rotting flesh, decomposing skin, tattered fins, recessed, bloody patches, loss of color, reduced mucus coating, loss of appetite, and listlessness.	Bacterial or Fungal Infection.	Diagnose ASAP. Quarantine and treat with appropriate antibiotic or broad-spectrum fungicide.
Slow growth, lack of appetite, faded colors, reduced level of activity, poor mucus coating.	Malnutrition or Vitamin Deficiency.	Vary the diet, add supplements such as vitamins, minerals, and bone meal to feed.
Huge size, lack of muscular definition, decreased levels of activity, increased breathing rate, insatiable appetite.	Obesity.	Reduce frequency of feedings and size of meals.
Huge size, tiny head, malformed jaws, insatiable appetite.	This moray was probably power-fed at some time.	Establish set feeding regimen and stick to it. Reduce overall amount of food offered.
Tiny "strings" of mucus hanging from body.	Slime-shedding.	Unsightly, but not dangerous. Introduce cleaner shrimp into aquarium.
Rapid breathing, irregular movements, loss of color, confusion, altered swimming habits.	Probably pH shock but may be more serious.	Check pH immediately and make any corrections to it at once if they are needed.

Rapid breathing, hanging at the top of the tank, involuntary muscle contractions, thrashing about, bumps on skin, loss of color, refusal to eat, holding head down, "side-swimming."	Nitrogenous Waste Pollution. Check Ammonia, nitrite, and nitrate immediately and take aggressive action to correct the problem if levels are high.	
Lumps under skin, sudden, unexplained refusal to feed, inability to swim upright. This behavior is not cured by standard treatments.	Probably a Tumor.	If operable, have the tumor removed by a certified veterinarian. If inoperable then you may want to explore euthanasia of the moray.

Resources

Magazines

Tropical Fish Hobbyist Magazine

The Leading Aquarium Magazine For Over Half a Century

Tropical Fish Hobbyist Magazine has been the source of accurate, up-to-the minute, fascinating information on every facet of the aquarium hobby including freshwater fish, marine aquaria, aquatic plants, mini-reefs, and ponds for over 50 years. *TFH* will take you to new heights with its informative articles and stunning photos. With thousands of fish, plants, and other aquatic animals available, the hobbyist needs levelheaded advice about their care, maintenance, and breeding. *TFH* authors have the knowledge and experience to help make your aquarium sensational.

P.O. Box 427

Neptune, NJ 07754-9989

For subscription information please visit: www.tfhmagazine.com

or call: 1-888-859-9034

Websites

Aquaria Central
www.aquariacentral.com

Fishbase
www.fishbase.org

Reef Central
www.reefcentral.com

Reefs.org
www.reefs.org

Tropical Resources
www.tropicalresources.net

Water Wolves
http://forums.waterwolves.com

Wet Web Media
www.wetwebmedia.com

Organizations

Marine Aquarium Council (MAC)

923 Nu'uanu Avenue

Honolulu, HI 96817

Telephone: (808) 550-8217

Fax: (808) 550-8317

E-mail: info@aquariumcouncil.com

www.aquariumcouncil.com

Marine Aquarium Societies of North America (MASNA)

Director of Memberships/Secretary:

Cheri Phillips

E-mail: cheri@uniqueensensations.com

www.masna.org

Index

Photo Credits

Bill Gately, 46
Bob Fenner, 30
Brian M. Scott, 76-77
Cathy Church, 44
Courtney Platt, 22, 105, 121 top left
G.R. Allen, 54, 71, 98
G.W. Lange, 47, 121 top right
James Fatherree, 17, 79, 100
Jason Prime, 41
John O'Malley, 82
John Randall, 107
Laurence Azoulay, 72

MP. & C. Piednoir, 8, 10, 60, 64, 86, 91, 96, 115
Mark Smith, 13, 32, 48, 88, 92, 94, 104, 106,
    108-110, 114, 116-117, 120, 121 bottom right,
    122 top left
Oliver Lucanus, 20, 51-52, 80, 101, 111, 122
    middle right & left photos,
R.G. Sprackland, 26
Richard Bell, 14
T.F.H. Archives, 24, 35-36, 38-39, 49, 56-58,
    62, 67-69, 74, 84, 99, 102-103, 112-113,
    118-119, 121 bottom left, 122 bottom right &
    left photos, 122 top right, 123 all photos